Accuracy of
and the New
International Version

Accuracy of Translation and the New International Version

The Primary Criterion in Evaluating Bible Versions

Robert P. Martin

The Banner of Truth Trust

THE BANNER OF TRUTH TRUST
3 Murrayfield Road, Edinburgh EH 12 6EL
PO Box 621, Carlisle, Pennsylvania 17013, USA

★

© Robert P Martin 1989
First published 1989
ISBN 0 85151 546 0

★

Typeset in 10½/12pt Linotron Plantin at The Spartan Press Limited,
Lymington, Hants
Reproduced, printed and bound in Great Britain by
The Camelot Press Ltd,
Southampton

CONTENTS

ABBREVIATIONS

ASV	American Standard Version (1901)
GNB	Good News Bible (1976)
KJV	King James Version (1611)
NASB	New American Standard Bible (1971)
NEB	New English Bible (1970)
NIV	New International Version (1985)
NKJV	New King James Version (1982)
RSV	Revised Standard Version (1952)

∾ I ∾

Why Write a Book on the Accuracy of the NIV?

One writer begins his work on Bible translations with this statement:

> The twentieth century Christian can be forgiven for feeling rather bewildered by the number and variety of Bible translations that have flooded the market. He may well want to know what the differences are between them and on what grounds he should make his choice. What makes a version 'one of the best' or places it amongst those which should be 'rejected'?[1]

My response to these observations is that the bewilderment in question extends to the pulpit as well as to the pew. We all have wrestled or are wrestling with the choice of a version for individual or corporate use. Pastors have been approached by their people seeking guidance as to the 'best' version to use. Quite often we find ourselves wishing that we had lived when the decision was relatively simple. Yet here we are with a wide variety of translations available, each making its own claim to the title 'best'.

At times it seems that we are in the midst of a popularity contest. The idea seems to be that the version which sells the most and which pleases the most people is the winner and, therefore, the 'best'. But should widespread popular appeal be the determining factor, especially in this day of shallow evangelicalism with its distaste for precise theological thinking? Could the very things which make some versions popular (and marketable) in the long

---

[1]Bob Sheehan, *Which Version Now?* (Haywards Heath, England: Carey Publications, n.d.), p. 1.

run produce even greater theological shallowness among evangelicals?

How are we to sort out the morass of information and misinformation? of advertising and promotional claims? of pronouncements by experts and counter-pronouncements by experts? Has the issue of Bible versions become so complex that we cannot now deal with it? Are we doomed to endless bewilderment? I do not think so.

Admittedly there are other issues to be considered in choosing a Bible translation for personal or corporate use; however, it seems to me that we must begin with the recognition that there is an overarching concern which dwarfs all other criteria in choosing a Bible version. What is the pre-eminent trait of a good Bible translation? The answer must be accuracy of translation. This is the overarching issue. It is with the criterion of accuracy that we must begin to make our choice of a Bible version.

Some readers may be disappointed that I am not proposing that our first concern must be the textual tradition being represented in translation (e.g., the Textus Receptus, the text of Westcott-Hort, the Majority Text, etc.). But Machen long ago reminded us that the difference between the manuscripts is 'infinitesimal in comparison with what they have in common'.[1] Although obviously it is important, the text issue has occupied a place larger than is warranted in the debate over Bible versions and has tended to overshadow the more critical issues of translation philosophy and accuracy of translation. As the result of exaggerated claims and unwarranted charges made by textual scholars, a cloud of suspicion now hangs over versions which, judged by other criteria, are excellent translations of the Bible.[2]

Why is accuracy of translation so important? Because the Bible is the Word of the living God. It is an utterly unique book. It is the inscripturated revelation to mankind of God's mind and will and the inspired record of His redemptive work. And this being so, there is no more important piece of literature in the world. Thus, the accuracy of the Bible's translation is of the utmost importance.

[1] J. Gresham Machen, *The Christian Faith in the Modern World* (New York: The Macmillan Company, 1936), p. 50.
[2] For a limited discussion of the text question, please see Appendix C: The Textus Receptus and the Text of the New Testament.

The concern for accuracy, however, deserves even greater consideration when we focus on the Bible's primary orientation. The Bible is a covenantal document (actually a combination of two such documents, the Old Testament and the New Testament). And it is primarily, though not exclusively, oriented to the people of God. The Bible primarily is the church's book, regulating her faith and practice. Milton Fisher reminds us that 'God's written revelation was not directed to or primarily intended for the general mass of unregenerate humanity . . . it was directed to a select group within humanity.'[1] Eugene Nida makes a similar point:

Bible translators . . . have often made quite a point of the fact that the language of the New Testament was Koine Greek, the language of 'the man in the street,' and hence a translation should speak to the man in the street. The truth of the matter is that many New Testament messages were not directed primarily to the man in the street, but to the man in the congregation.[2]

No other claim on the Bible supersedes the church's claim. The church's need of an accurate and reliable standard of faith and practice supersedes every other concern. Indeed, the church has a right to demand that her need must occupy first place in the mind of the translator. The translator must remember that he is a servant of God translating God's book for the benefit of God's people. He has no right placing any other concern ahead of the church's need for accurate translations.

As the title of this book indicates, the focus of our study will be on the *New International Version*. The reason for concentrating on the NIV is twofold.

First, according to a publisher's release, the goal for the NIV is 'to do for our time what the King James Version did for its day'. Undoubtedly, Zondervan Bible Publishers hopes that the NIV will become the standard version of the English-speaking world and apparently they have spared no expense in promoting it. And by all appearances they are succeeding. According to a recent full-page advertisement in *Christianity Today* (under the heading 'New

[1]Milton Fisher, 'Normative Principles for Bible Translating', in *The New Testament Student and Bible Translation*, ed. John H. Skilton (Phillipsburg, New Jersey: Presbyterian and Reformed Publishing Company, 1978), p. 20.

[2]Eugene A. Nida, *Toward a Science of Translating* (Leiden: E. J. Brill, 1964), p. 170.

International Version Translation Takes Over First Place in Bible Sales'), Zondervan reported that by the end of 1986 'the New International Version had overtaken the familiar King James Version as this country's [i.e., the USA's] best-selling translation of the Bible'. Surely such a milestone warrants a second look at the NIV.

Second, the NIV has been promoted as an accurate translation of the Bible. In the version's preface, the Committee on Bible Translation affirms, 'The first concern of the translators has been the accuracy of the translation and its fidelity to the thought of the biblical writers.'[1] With the passing of time, however, in many quarters there has been a growing concern about the NIV's accuracy as a translation. I share this concern and feel very uneasy about the long-term effects of the use of the NIV in the churches. Although we will address our subject within the boundaries of a consideration of the wider question of translation philosophy, our primary question is whether the NIV is accurate enough as a translation to warrant its becoming the standard version of the English-speaking world. Or we might frame the question another way. The church needs an accurate translation of the Bible as her guide in faith and practice; does the NIV meet the need of the church?

While to some it may seem ungracious and even argumentative to find fault with a work undertaken with such great devotion, let me assure the reader that I have no desire to cast aspersions on the character or motives of the NIV translators. The common witness is that they are men of unimpeachable Christian character and devotion to the Word of God; and I have no reason to dispute that testimony. My sole concern is the product which was produced by their labours.

The NIV has undergone revision since its first edition. The latest edition available when my research began was the text published in *The NIV Study Bible* (1985). My research was confined to that edition. Furthermore, my remarks are limited to the New Testament. My knowledge of Hebrew is not such that I can remark with equal confidence on the translation accuracy of the NIV Old Testament. Others more qualified must make that judgment. I must say, however, that if the NIV New Testament is

[1] *The NIV Study Bible* (Grand Rapids: Zondervan Bible Publishers, 1985), p. xi.

seriously lacking in translation accuracy, that fact alone would warrant rejecting the NIV as the standard for determining the faith and practice of the churches.

The subject will be treated in the following fashion. In Chapter 2 the difference between the two primary translation philosophies, formal equivalence and dynamic equivalence, will be explained. In Chapter 3 we will look at the question of translation philosophy in relation to the nature of the Bible's inspiration. In Chapters 4 and 5 we will examine dynamic elements in the NIV New Testament. In Chapter 6 we will seek to draw some conclusions concerning the accuracy of the NIV as a translation of the Word of God.

∽ 2 ∽

What Translation Philosophy Produced the NIV?

In order to evaluate the accuracy of the NIV as a translation, it is necessary to understand the philosophy of translation which produced it. Different methods of translation, of course, produce different kinds of translations. For example, the philosophy behind the American Standard Version is radically different from that behind the Good News Bible (Today's English Version); and, thus, the resultant translations are radically different as well.[1]

The task of the Bible translator is to communicate the content of the biblical texts (originally written in Hebrew, Aramaic, and Greek) in the native language of the readers for whom the translation is being prepared (in our case, in English). The translator is concerned with equivalence, that is, he is concerned that his finished translation communicates accurately what the original author wrote. The issue, of course, is the method of doing this most effectively. What method or philosophy of translation should the translator use?

Nida asserts that 'there are fundamentally two different types of equivalence', two basic orientations, 'two poles of translating' – formal equivalence and dynamic equivalence.[2] Now while the

[1]The contrast is evident virtually anywhere one turns; however, compare in the ASV and the GNB the rendering of the familiar and important words of the apostle Paul at Romans 3:19–26. Speaking of the ASV (and of its companion, the English Revised Version), Nida comments, 'These versions are as literal as they can be and still make sense – the result of well-defined principles aimed at producing just such a translation.' Nida, *Toward a Science of Translating*, p. 20.

[2]Nida, *Toward a Science of Translating*, pp. 159–60. Nida later substituted the terms 'formal correspondence' and 'functional equivalence'. See Jan

existing English translations evidence differing levels of consistency in the application of either formal equivalence or dynamic equivalence, nevertheless each one (either consciously or unconsciously) is oriented to one philosophy or the other. In the paragraphs which follow, we will examine the philosophies of formal equivalence and dynamic equivalence; and, then, we will try to ascertain the philosophical orientation of the NIV.

When we ask what method of translating best communicates the content of the original text, formal equivalence translators answer that the content of the original is best communicated when the translator consciously tries to parallel closely the linguistic form (i.e., the structure, grammar, and exact wording) of the original. Dynamic equivalence translators, on the other hand, answer that the best way is to use the most natural form of the language of the reader (i.e., giving priority to the structure, grammar, and idiomatic expressions of contemporary English), whether or not this closely parallels the linguistic form of the original text. Albeit with differing levels of consistency in application, the formal equivalence method basically was followed by the translators of the King James Version, the American Standard Version (and the English Revised Version), the New American Standard Bible, and the New King James Version. Dynamic equivalence was the method followed, for example, in the production of the Good News Bible and the New English Bible.

As noted above, the formal equivalence translator, when translating the content of the original text into English, tries to

---

de Waard and Eugene A. Nida, *From One Language to Another: Functional Equivalence in Bible Translating* (Nashville: Thomas Nelson Publishers, 1986), pp. vii, 36. Price prefers the term 'complete equivalence' to 'formal equivalence', noting that the word 'formal' has been criticized as indicating a concern for form but not for meaning. James D. Price, *Complete Equivalence in Bible Translation* (Nashville: Thomas Nelson Publishers, 1987), p. 37. Beekman and Callow prefer the terms 'literal' and 'idiomatic'. They argue, 'If its [i.e., a translation's] form corresponds more to the form of the original text, it is classed as *literal*; if its form corresponds more to the form of the receptor language, then it is classed as *idiomatic*.' John Beekman and John Callow, *Translating the Word of God* (Grand Rapids: Zondervan Publishing House, 1974), p. 21. In this study, the terms 'formal equivalence' and 'dynamic equivalence' will be retained. I believe that these terms are still the most accurate and the most widely used.

preserve the form of the original text as far as possible. With this philosophical orientation, the translator is concerned that the elements of the finished translation match as closely as possible the elements of the original text. He is concerned that paragraph corresponds to paragraph, sentence to sentence, clause to clause, phrase to phrase, and word to word. The formal equivalence philosophy or method of translating attempts to say 'what' the original text says by retaining 'how' it says it (as far as English grammar allows). Although clear English expression does not always allow the formal equivalence translator to do so, he tries not to adjust the idioms which the original writer used; rather, he attempts to render them more or less literally, so that the reader may be able to perceive something of the way in which the original document employed local linguistic and cultural elements to convey ideas.

Because of their methodological orientation, formal equivalence translators frequently are accused of being concerned with preserving the form of the original text rather than its meaning. This is a caricature. As Price observes, 'Structural information is as much a part of the message as the information contained in the words themselves.'[1] The formal equivalence method attempts to transfer (as far as is possible) the structural information of the message as well as the general idea or meaning of the words.

In contrast to formal equivalence translators, dynamic equivalence translators focus attention not so much on the form of the original text as on the response of the modern reader. A dynamic equivalence translation has been described as one concerning which a modern reader could say, 'That is just the way we would say it.' As can be seen, in contrast to the philosophy of formal equivalence, the philosophy of dynamic equivalence definitely has moved in the direction of paraphrase.

The dynamic equivalence translation is based on the principle of 'equivalent effect' rather than on the principle of 'formal linguistic equivalence'. By 'equivalent effect' is meant that the translator tries to discern what the 'impact' of the original would have been on the original readers and then he tries to use the English style and idiom which will make a similar (if not an identical) impact on the modern reader. De Waard and Nida assert that in the dynamic equivalence method, 'The translation process has been defined on

[1]Price, p. 37.

the basis that the receptors of a translation should comprehend the translated text to such an extent that they can understand how the original receptors must have understood the original text.'[1] The main concern of dynamic equivalence, therefore, is not formal linguistic correspondence but correspondence of thought or idea.

Every translation of the Bible is a mixture of formal and dynamic elements. On the one hand, since no two languages are exactly identical, either in the meanings given to corresponding words or in the ways such words are arranged in phrases and sentences, it stands to reason that there can be no absolutely formal correspondence between languages. Therefore, there can be no absolutely 'literal' translations. There are occasions when the differences between the biblical languages and English are such that the formal equivalence translator cannot preserve in translation the precise grammatical structure of the original; and, in such cases, accommodation must be made to the English idiom to the degree necessary for clear communication.[2] On the other hand, all dynamic equivalence translations must have at least some formal relationship to the original texts; otherwise they would not qualify as translations at all.

Since it is true that dynamic elements are found in all the available English versions, some might argue that the difference between them is merely a matter of the degree of liberty taken to make the content of the original text clear to the modern reader. In one sense I suppose that this is true; but I also believe that it is an over-simplification. If this is an accurate assessment of the current situation, then one would expect that the line between the existing formal equivalence and dynamic equivalence translations would be blurred completely. This, of course, is not the case. As Beekman and Callow observe, 'Even though there are few, if any, translations that are completely literal or completely idiomatic, each has been produced with one or the other approach in mind.'[3]

Although within each grouping (formal equivalence or dynamic equivalence) the differences are a matter of the degree of consistency with the method of translation being used, the differences between the groupings themselves are a matter of

[1]De Waard and Nida, p. 36.
[2]For example, the Greek third person imperative has no exact parallel in English.
[3]Beekman and Callow, p. 21.

method itself. This means that although a translation, consciously produced using the method of formal equivalence, may have some dynamic elements *out of necessity*; yet, nevertheless, it is far removed from all translations produced on the basis of the philosophy of dynamic equivalence. Conversely, although a dynamic equivalence translation will *out of necessity* have some formal relationship to the original texts; yet, nevertheless, it is far removed from all translations produced on the basis of the philosophy of formal equivalence. The difference is one of kind, not just one of degree.

The American Standard Version clearly was produced using the method of formal equivalence. And whereas there are dynamic elements found in it, no student of the original languages would confuse it with the Good News Bible, which plainly was produced using the method of dynamic equivalence. The difference between them clearly is one of kind, not just of degree.

The Revised Standard Version is a curious production. The revisers apparently were committed to the philosophy of dynamic equivalence; and, I believe, had they been producing a completely new translation, they would have produced something like the Good News Bible. But they were revising the American Standard Version, the most literal of the formal equivalence translations. Bound by a commitment to the ASV, but philosophically committed to a radically different philosophy from that which lay behind the version being revised, they produced a document which is philosophically schizophrenic.

The New American Standard Bible also sought to revise the ASV into modern English; and the revisers largely succeeded, although they made room for more dynamic elements than the ASV translators had. The preface to the NASB states, 'When it was felt that the word-for-word literalness of the ASV was unacceptable to the modern reader, a change was made in the direction of a more current English idiom.'[1] According to the publishers of the New King James Version, the NKJV was produced on the basis of 'complete equivalence' (i.e., formal equivalence); indeed, Price's monograph (*Complete Equivalence in Bible Translation*) is currently being distributed by Thomas Nelson Publishers as part of its campaign promoting the NKJV.

[1]*New American Standard Bible* (Glendale, California: Regal Books, 1971), p. vii.

What Translation Philosophy Produced the NIV?

Where does the NIV fit into the picture philosophically? What is its philosophical orientation? In *The Story of the New International Version*, published by the International Bible Society, the Committee on Bible Translation (the governing body of the NIV project) states:

Broadly speaking, there are several methods of translation: the concordant one, which ranges from literalism to the comparative freedom of the King James Version and even more of the Revised Standard Version, both of which follow the syntactical structure of the Hebrew and Greek texts as far as is compatible with good English; the paraphrastic one, in which the translator restates the gist of the text in his own words; and the method of equivalence, in which the translator seeks to understand as fully as possible what the biblical writers had to say (a criterion common, of course, to the careful use of any method) and then tries to find its closest equivalent in contemporary usage. In its more advanced form this is spoken of as dynamic equivalence, in which the translator seeks to express the meaning as the biblical writers would if they were writing in English today. All these methods have their values when responsibly used.

As for the NIV, its method is an eclectic one with the emphasis for the most part on a flexible use of concordance and equivalence, but with a minimum of literalism, paraphrase, or outright dynamic equivalence. In other words, the NIV stands on middle ground – by no means the easiest position to occupy.[1]

It is my desire to be fair to the NIV translators; however, their statement of translation philosophy is confusing. On the one hand, they admittedly were not operating with a consistent philosophy of formal equivalence (which they call the 'concordant' method), for they say, 'As for the NIV, its method is an eclectic one with the emphasis for the most part on a flexible use of concordance and equivalence.' On the other hand, they are concerned that their work not be associated closely with the philosophy of dynamic equivalence; admitting, however, that they made use of the method of 'equivalence'. But the method of 'equivalence' (as they define it) is not different in kind from the method of 'dynamic equivalence'. At most the difference is one of degree, not of kind, since 'dynamic equivalence' is merely the 'more advanced form' of the method of 'equivalence'.

[1] *The Story of the New International Version* (East Brunswick, New Jersey: International Bible Society, 1978), pp. 12–13.

The term 'equivalence', of course, used without any qualifying adjective, is ambiguous. The question is, What kind of equivalence? Unless a distinction in kind, and not just in degree, can be made, the so-called method of 'equivalence' is nothing more than an application of 'dynamic equivalence'.

The Committee is accurate in describing the method used in the production of the NIV as 'an eclectic one'; however, it is not accurate to say that the NIV contains 'a minimum . . . of outright dynamic equivalence'. Although the NIV is not as 'dynamic' as the Good News Bible or the New English Bible, nevertheless the NIV translators have been heavily influenced by the dynamic equivalence philosophy of translation. Indeed, the NIV has more in common with the dynamic equivalence translations than with the formal equivalence translations. I believe that the evidence given in Chapters 4 and 5 ('Dynamic Elements in the NIV New Testament') will sustain this conclusion.

3

Translation and the Nature of the Bible's Inspiration

In the next chapter we will take up an examination of dynamic elements in the NIV New Testament. Before turning to that subject, however, another topic must occupy our attention.

The Scriptures claim that they are 'inspired of God', i.e., 'God-breathed' (*2 Timothy 3:16*). It is assumed that the vast majority of Bible translators acknowledge in some sense the Bible's inspiration. The Bible is a special book to them and they have given many years of labour to its study. As a general rule, however, the translator's view of the nature of the Bible's inspiration greatly influences his philosophy of translation. That this statement is beyond dispute may be seen from the remarkable way in which modern Bible translators to a large degree have followed the paths cut by the modern debate over the Bible's inspiration and authority.

I shall not here enter into a survey of the various views of biblical inspiration nor present the evidence for the view which I regard as the correct one; the standard works on the doctrine of the Word have done this carefully already.[1] It must suffice for me to say that the weight of the evidence in favour of verbal-plenary inspiration so preponderates that the doctrine has never even begun to be

[1]See, for example, Benjamin B. Warfield, *The Inspiration and Authority of the Bible* (Phillipsburg, New Jersey: The Presbyterian and Reformed Publishing Co., 1948); Thomas A. Thomas, *The Doctrine of the Word of God* (Nutley, New Jersey: The Presbyterian and Reformed Publishing Co., 1977); Edward J. Young, *Thy Word is Truth* (Edinburgh: The Banner of Truth Trust, 1980); Carl F. H. Henry, ed., *Revelation and the Bible* (Grand Rapids: Baker Book House, 1958).

overthrown, the claims of liberalism and neo-orthodoxy notwithstanding. The Bible is inspired in such a way that its very words are inspired (i.e., 'verbal' inspiration); and that inspiration extends to all the words of Scripture (i.e., 'plenary' inspiration). The nature of the Bible's inspiration is such that what it says is what God has said.

The so-called 'dynamic' view of inspiration, on the other hand, argues that God inspired the thoughts of the biblical writers but left them to express those thoughts or ideas in their own words. In accordance with this view it has been argued that as long as we have the general ideas, then the exact words do not matter; and, thus, as long as the translator captures the biblical writer's 'idea', then he is free to express that idea in whatever words he chooses. The dynamic method of translation corresponds to the dynamic view of inspiration.

The dynamic view of inspiration, of course, is wrong at its root. To my knowledge none of its proponents have succeeded in explaining by what method God conveyed ideas to the minds of the biblical writers without using words, which are the building blocks of thought. Human thought is both verbal and visual, that is, we think in terms of verbal and visual imagery. Since most of the great doctrines of the faith, however, are not capable of visual expression (e.g., justification), one is left with the inescapable conclusion that these 'ideas' came to the minds of the inspired writers in verbal (word) form. This agrees of course with the Bible's own claim. Paul clearly asserted, 'We received, not the spirit of the world, but the Spirit which is from God; that we might know the things that were freely given to us of God; which things also we speak, not *in words* which man's wisdom teacheth, but *which the Spirit teacheth*' (*1 Corinthians 2:12–13*). It is also clear that the biblical writers hang important doctrinal propositions on individual words, verb tenses, etc. The exact words are, therefore, of great importance.

The fact that the Bible teaches a doctrine of verbal-plenary inspiration must influence the work of the translator. An inspiration that extends to the divine choice of the words can only imply that God is concerned with much more than general ideas. It is clear that God intends that we understand Him exactly. The translator must keep in mind that he is dealing with truth exactly expressed. His job, therefore, is to express the same truth as exactly as possible in the language of his people, to express in the most precise form possible the same message in the vocabulary and grammatical forms of the target language. As Iain Murray has said:

When the Bible is being translated, its own doctrine as to its verbal inspiration imposes limitations on the translators' function. The Scripture teaches us that, as God's word written, its form as well as its thought is inspired. The translator of Scripture has, therefore, above all else, to *follow* the text: it is not his business to interpret it or to explain it.[1]

Though direct correspondence cannot be demonstrated in every case, the general tendency has been to find dynamic equivalence translation associated with heterodox views of biblical inspiration and authority. James Moffatt, for example, admittedly translated 'freed from the influence of the theory of verbal inspiration'.[2] Robert Bratcher, one of the main translators of the Good News Bible, vigorously criticized belief in biblical inerrancy: 'Only wilful ignorance or intellectual dishonesty can account for the claim that the Bible is inerrant and infallible. To qualify this absurd claim by adding "with respect to the autographs (original manuscripts)" is a bit of sophistry, a specious attempt to justify a patent error.'[3] Where such views are held, it is no mystery that

---

[1] Iain Murray, 'Which Version? A Continuing Debate', in *The New Testament Student and Bible Translation*, p. 132.

[2] James Moffatt, *The New Testament: A New Translation* (1913), p. vii.

[3] The source of these remarks is a printed formal press release from Baptist Press, the official news agency of the Southern Baptist Convention, dated 25 March 1981 (by-line by Dan Martin). Bratcher's remarks are from an address on the authority of the Bible delivered at a national seminar of the Southern Baptist Christian Life Commission on the use and abuse of authority. The following are further specimens of Bratcher's comments regarding the inspiration and authority of the Bible: 'No truth-loving, God-respecting, Christ-honoring believer should be guilty of such heresy. To invest the Bible with the qualities of inerrancy and infallibility is to idolatrize it, to transform it into a false god.' 'No one seriously claims that all the words of the Bible are the very words of God. If someone does so it is only because that person is not willing thoroughly to explore its implications.' 'Even words spoken by Jesus in Aramaic in the thirties of the first century and preserved in writing in Greek, 35 to 50 years later, do not necessarily wield compelling or authentic authority over us today. The locus of scriptural authority is not the words themselves. It is Jesus Christ as THE Word of God who is the authority for us to be and to do.'

translators employ a dynamic equivalence philosophy of translation.

The tendency to de-emphasize or even to deny altogether verbal-plenary inspiration has an affinity to the dynamic equivalence method of translation, for the method itself elevates the primacy of ideas over the primacy of the exact words of the original text. Nida recognized this when he said:

For the most part, it [neo-orthodox theology] conceives of inspiration primarily in terms of the response of the receptor, and places less emphasis on what happened to the source at the time of writing. An oversimplified statement of this new view is reflected in the often quoted expression, 'The Scriptures are inspired because they inspire me.' Such a concept of inspiration means, however, that attention is inevitably shifted from the details of wording in the original to the means by which the same message can be effectively communicated to present-day readers. Those who espouse the traditional, orthodox view of inspiration quite naturally focus attention on the presumed readings of the 'autographs.' The result is that, directly or indirectly, they often tend to favor quite close, literal renderings as the best way of preserving the inspiration of the writer by the Holy Spirit. On the other hand, those who hold the neo-orthodox view, or who have been influenced by it, tend to be freer in their translating; as they see it, since the original document inspired its readers because it spoke meaningfully to them, only an equally meaningful translation can have this same power to inspire present-day receptors. It would be quite wrong, however, to assume that all those who emphasize fully meaningful translations necessarily hold to a neo-orthodox view of inspiration; for those who have combined orthodox theology with deep evangelistic or missionary convictions have been equally concerned with the need for making translations entirely meaningful.[1]

In order for the verbal and plenary inspiration of the Bible to be properly acknowledged in the work of translation, the primary unit of translation must be the word, not just the idea. Any method of translation which departs from that commitment is in serious conflict with the doctrine of verbal-plenary inspiration; for that doctrine proposes that inspiration extends to the individual words of the original text (so that it is 'verbal' inspiration) and to all of the individual words of the original text (so that it is 'plenary' inspiration). Plainly speaking, the formal equivalence method of

---

[1]Nida, *Toward a Science of Translating*, p. 27.

translation is philosophically committed to regarding and guarding the individual words of the original text as the primary units of translation; the dynamic equivalence method is not. Thus, the further the translator departs from formal equivalence in his work, the less compatible his method and ultimately the finished product become with the orthodox doctrine of biblical inspiration and authority.

᎗ 4 ᎗

Dynamic Elements in the NIV New Testament (1)

In a sense, to this point I have asked the reader to consider the question of translation philosophy primarily on the theoretical level. My purpose, however, was not to leave the reader with the impression that differences in translation philosophy have no practical importance; rather, my aim has been to erect the framework needed for the consideration of the subject of this chapter and the next, that is, a consideration of dynamic elements in the NIV New Testament.

A difference in translation method has tremendous significance on the practical level. When the reader picks up a Bible version produced using the method of dynamic equivalence, he finds features in it which are quite different from the features which he finds in a translation produced using the method of formal equivalence. The purpose of this chapter and the next is to note seven characteristics of dynamic equivalence translations and to observe how the NIV, albeit in varying degrees, displays these same features.

I. THE ELIMINATION OF COMPLEX GRAMMATICAL STRUCTURES

Because it seeks to stay as close to the form of the original as possible, generally speaking the formal equivalence translation will reflect more closely the grammatical structure of the original, including even complex levels of subordination. Dynamic equivalence translators, on the other hand, tend to divide complex sentences into a series of simple sentences.

I recall being required at seminary to produce a grammatical diagram of Ephesians 1:3–14, a passage which is a single complex sentence in the Greek text. This project consumed much time and paper; however, it was a very profitable use of both. The diagram revealed the complexity and interrelatedness of Paul's argument, as well as the hierarchy of concerns within it. Diagramming revealed, for example, that Paul's primary concern is contained in the words, 'Blessed be the God and Father of our Lord Jesus Christ'; everything else in the passage is subordinate to and supportive of this affirmation. While a formal equivalence translation of this passage certainly does not display the grammatical structure as dramatically as a grammatical diagram does, nevertheless to a large degree it likewise allows the modern reader to see the close interrelatedness of Paul's argument and the hierarchy of concerns within it. To the degree that translations move away from treating such complex passages as single grammatical entities (i.e., by breaking them up into separate sentences, thus rendering as coordinate that which is subordinate in the original), to that degree they misrepresent the original and mislead the reader. Note in the chart below how differently the various translations treat examples of single complex sentences.

Number of Sentences

Eph. 1:3–14		*2 Thess. 1:3–10*	
ASV	1	ASV	1
KJV	3	KJV	1
NKJV	3	NKJV	2
NASB	4	NASB	4
RSV	6	RSV	4
NIV	8	NIV	8
GNB	15	GNB	9

Eph. 1:15–21		*Acts 1:1–5*	
ASV	1	ASV	1
KJV	1	KJV	2
NKJV	1	NKJV	2
RSV	1	NASB	3
NASB	3	RSV	3
NIV	4	NIV	4
GNB	5	GNB	6

	1 Cor. 5:3–5		*Heb. 1:1–4*
ASV	1	ASV	1
KJV	1	KJV	1
NKJV	2	NKJV	1
NASB	2	NASB	3
RSV	2	RSV	3
GNB	2	NIV	4
NIV	3	GNB	5

Clearly, as these examples show, in this area the NIV has more in common with the philosophy of dynamic equivalence than with the philosophy of formal equivalence.

It is often objected that with their so-called 'wooden literalism', formal equivalence translations confront the reader with difficult grammatical structures and, thus, with a lack of clarity.[1] To this charge we answer that indeed in formal equivalence translations the reader encounters many passages that are complex grammatically. We do not, however, encounter passages which cannot be understood by the average literate adult Christian who is willing to make an effort at studying them.

It is true that formal equivalence translations do not read as easily as modern newspapers, gossip magazines, or pulp novels; but this should not surprise us. The Bible is not a pulp novel but the Word of the living God. Unlike the modern newspaper, the Bible was never meant to yield the fullness of its message to those who are only willing to expend the absolute minimum of effort necessary. Formal equivalence translations admittedly require more effort on the part of the reader, that is, more study, more investigation, more thought, more prayer; but surely the importance of the subject matter warrants the greater effort expended.

---

[1]Commenting on 1 Corinthians 5:3–5, which is one sentence in the Greek text, Edwin Palmer complained, 'One problem of the KJV is that its sentences ramble on and on and are too complicated to figure out.' Edwin H. Palmer, 'Isn't the King James Version Good Enough? (The KJV and the NIV Compared)', in *The NIV: The Making of a Contemporary Translation*, ed. Kenneth L. Barker (Grand Rapids: Zondervan Publishing House, 1986), p. 148. The alleged problem, of course, is not with the KJV but with the original Greek text.

It is true that many have been short-changed in their opportunity to acquire good reading skills. It is fashionable to place the blame on the educational experts who decided that an entire generation of students did not need to learn phonics as a basis for reading skills. But is it enough to place blame? At some point those who were short-changed by the educational system must cease to lament the wrong done to them and must take personal responsibility for bettering their reading skills. No matter how simply we translate, we can never produce a Bible for the functionally illiterate, or even for the marginally literate, and still remain faithful to the structure of what is, by any standard, a very complex book.

I fear that much of the cry for a translation which requires little effort to understand is rooted in the itch of our age for instant gratification. Many in a generation raised in the climate of instant everything (instant coffee, instant potatoes, instant-on radio and television, microwave ovens, no-iron fabrics, computerized instant banking services – the list is virtually endless) have come to regard instant spirituality and instant Bible knowledge as their birthright. The idea that one must labour over the Word of God in order to mine its gold is a revolutionary concept to many in our day.

Although the message of the Bible is in one sense quite simple, yet in another sense it is profound and complex. Indeed, the Bible itself is composed of sixty-six very complex documents. Simply put, the complexity of the formal equivalence translations is not the product of the translator but of the Spirit of God who inspired the originals. Was it formal equivalence translators who made Ephesians 1:3–14 one complex sentence or was it written by Paul under the guidance of the Spirit of God? It was Paul. And ultimately, it was the Spirit of God, was it not? Moreover, we cannot assume that the complex grammatical structures of the original texts constitute a uniquely modern problem and presented no difficulty to the original readers. It is worthy of note that even the apostle Peter observed that Paul's writings contained 'some things hard to be understood' (*2 Peter 3:16*); nevertheless, he does not charge his fellow apostle with writing things 'impossible to be understood' nor does he suggest that the difficulties be removed. Thus by preserving complex grammatical structures, the formal equivalence translator is not disregarding the need for clarity; he is simply being faithful to what God has given by inspiration.

2. THE ADDITION OF WORDS IN TRANSLATION

At times translators add words which are not found in the original text but which are deemed necessary to express the sense of the original. In some cases this is done in the interest of clear English expression; in other cases the interpretive opinions of the translators lie behind the added words. In all fairness we must acknowledge that this is not just a phenomenon of dynamic equivalence translations but of formal equivalence translations as well; however, also in all fairness we must recognize that this is a much more frequent phenomenon in dynamic equivalence translations, arising undoubtedly from the more paraphrastic and interpretive style which the concern for 'equivalent effect' produces. Moreover, as a general rule (although not always, as the examples immediately following make clear) the formal equivalence translation uses italics to indicate words supplied by the translator but missing in the original text; whereas, also as a general rule, the dynamic equivalence translator uses no such convention.

Two passages, both employing the word *puroō*, illustrate the phenomena which we have been describing. The verb *puroō* literally means 'to burn'; however, at both 1 Corinthians 7:9 and 2 Corinthians 11:29, the immediate contexts indicate that the word should be understood metaphorically.

At 1 Corinthians 7:9 the KJV (along with the ASV and the NASB) translates literally that it is better to marry than 'to burn'. With but few exceptions, however, commentators have agreed that the context demands that we understand Paul as saying that 'marriage, with all its inconveniences, is much better than to burn with impure and lustful desires'.[1] Several translations display a sensitivity to this consensus of opinion. The RSV has 'to be aflame with passion'; the GNB and NIV have 'to burn with passion'. The NASB, which gives the literal rendering in the text, has 'burn with passion' in a marginal notation. The NKJV also has 'to burn *with passion*', but 'with passion' is in italics, indicating to the reader that the words are supplied by the translators.

At 2 Corinthians 11:29 *puroō* occurs again, albeit with a different sense than at 1 Corinthians 7:9. Again the KJV (along with the ASV) translates literally, 'who is offended [caused to stumble,

[1]Matthew Henry, *Commentary on the Whole Bible* (reprint ed., McLean, Virginia: MacDonald Publishing Company, n.d.), 6:537.

ASV], and I burn not?' Unlike the use of *puroō* at 1 Corinthians 7:9, however, there is no consensus of opinion among interpreters. Nevertheless, some translations include interpretive opinions, albeit without the use of italics. The NASB has 'who is led into sin without my intense concern?' in the text; but the translators call attention to the literal rendering 'and I do not burn' in a marginal notation. The NKJV has 'who is made to stumble, and I do not burn with indignation?'; but the words 'with indignation' are added without italics. The RSV, which shares the interpretive opinion of the NKJV, is more paraphrastic, with 'who is made to fall, and I am not indignant?' The GNB has 'when someone is led into sin, I am filled with distress'. The NIV has 'who is led into sin, and I do not inwardly burn?'; but the word 'inwardly' is added without italics.

The example of 2 Corinthians 11:29 is particularly helpful because it reflects not only the ordinary procedure of dynamic equivalence translations but also the inconsistency of some formal equivalence translations with their ordinary procedure. On the one hand, the dynamic equivalence translations are true to form. They are either so paraphrastic as to make the use of italics impossible (e.g., GNB, RSV) or they do not use italics where it would be possible to do so (e.g., 'and I do not *inwardly* burn', NIV). On the other hand, at 2 Corinthians 11:29 the NASB and the NKJV are inconsistent not only with the philosophy of formal equivalence but also with themselves. When we compare how these versions treat 1 Corinthians 7:9 and 2 Corinthians 11:29, this is clear. At 1 Corinthians 7:9 the correct interpretation of *puroō* is relatively certain (i.e., to burn with passion); yet there (and rightly so) both the NASB and the NKJV are very conservative in their renderings. The NASB gives a literal rendering in the text and restricts interpretation to a marginal note; the NKJV adds 'with passion' only in italics, indicating that the words are supplied by the translator. At 2 Corinthians 11:29, however, the correct interpretation of *puroō* clearly is in doubt, with some opting for 'intense concern', others for 'indignation', and others for being 'filled with distress'. Yet here, where one would think that a cautious and conservative rendering clearly is called for, the NASB reverses the procedure used at 1 Corinthians 7:9 and gives interpretive opinion in the text, while relegating the literal meaning to a marginal note. The NKJV likewise reverses the procedure used at 1 Corinthians 7:9 and adds 'with indignation' without italics and thus with no indication to the reader that these words have been added by the translator.

In calling attention to the inconsistency of formal equivalence translations with reference to the use of italics, I am seeking to be fair in my criticism. In what follows I will criticize the NIV for failing to use italics where words have been added by the translators. When I do so, it is with the awareness that the formal equivalence translations in a limited number of instances are guilty of the same thing.

The NIV translators explained the lack of italics in their version this way: 'To achieve clarity the translators sometimes supplied words not in the original texts but required by the context. If there was uncertainty about such material, it is enclosed in brackets.'[1] Apparently the NIV translators felt that they had achieved a high degree of certainty in their additions, for to the best of my knowledge only eight times do they use brackets in all of the New Testament (i.e., *Luke 11:41*; *John 8:24, 28*; *12:7*; *Acts 19:15*; *Galatians 2:4*; *4:17*; *2 Thessalonians 2:3*).[2] Even granting a high degree of certainty in such matters, however, one must question the propriety of passing on to the reader (without the use of a convention such as italics or brackets) one's conjectures as to 'words not in the original texts but required by the context' to 'achieve clarity'. Should not all such conjectures be clearly marked so that the reader can judge them for himself?

Except at the few places noted by brackets, the NIV translators give no hint that liberties have been taken with the addition of words. The examples which appear below are only from passages where the NIV translation was literal enough to allow the determination to be made that specific words could have been italicized (or bracketed) to reflect the addition of words not found in the original text. At many places the NIV is so paraphrastic that a convention such as italics or brackets would be meaningless as far as indicating verbal deviations from the formal linguistic pattern of the original text. Indeed, once a concern for close formal correspondence is abandoned, the use of italics becomes generally impossible.

[1] *The NIV Study Bible*, p. xiii.

[2] These eight places were discovered by visual inspection while reading through the NIV New Testament. The half-brackets are quite small; and it is possible that my eyes passed over others unnoticed.

In some cases the NIV translators have added words, yet without a shift of meaning. While this is less serious than the addition of words which change the sense of the original or point the reader to a favoured interpretation, nevertheless in both cases the translator is obligated to inform the reader that liberty has been taken with the text. The following are a few examples of places where the NIV has added words without italics or brackets, yet (in my opinion) with no significant change in meaning:

Text	*Words supplied but not original*
Matt. 13:44	again
Matt. 17:20	small as
Matt. 23:30	shedding
Mark 1:4	and so
Luke 18:14	before God
John 16:8	of guilt
Acts 3:19	to God (but cf. 26:20)
Acts 11:23	the evidence of
Rom. 1:5	to call people
Rom. 4:25	over to death
Rom. 5:2	now (but cf. *nun* at 5:9, 11)
Rom. 11:11	beyond recovery
Eph. 3:6	with Israel
Phil. 2:4	only
1 Pet. 2:11	in the world
Rev. 1:6	to serve
Rev. 7:10	belongs

There are other places, however, where the addition of words changes the sense of the original or points the reader to a favoured interpretation. This, of course, is a more serious matter. Therefore, instead of merely listing these examples (as above), a word of explanation will be given with each one.

At Acts 5:20 the text reads literally 'all the words of this life'. The NIV reads 'the full message of this new life'. Our concern is the word 'new', added without warrant from the original text and without italics or brackets. The word 'new', however, clearly adds to the sense of the original and should either be omitted or at least identified as not original.

Matthew 23:32 literally may be rendered, 'Fill up then the measure of your fathers'. The NIV adds the interpretive words 'of the sin' without brackets, so that the verse reads, 'Fill up, then, the measure of the sin of your forefathers'. The NASB, however, suggests 'of the guilt' (in italics); while the NEB has, 'Go on then, finish off what your fathers began', offering as a marginal alternative, 'You too must come up to your fathers' standards'. It is also possible, looking at verse 33 ('how shall you escape the judgment of hell?'), that we are to understand Jesus as saying that the scribes and Pharisees will fill up 'with divine wrath' the measure of judgment to be poured out upon them, a judgment far more severe than that which came upon even their wicked forefathers.

At Matthew 13:32 the NIV translators apparently are trying to rescue Jesus from scientific embarrassment when he calls the mustard seed 'less than all seeds' (ASV). Adding the word 'your' without brackets, the NIV reads 'the smallest of all your seeds'. In a similar case, lest Jesus appear to be rude to his mother by calling her 'woman' (*gunai*), the NIV has 'Dear woman' at John 2:4, although 'Dear' is not in brackets. Apparently they were content, however, in one of the most tender scenes recorded in the Gospels, to let Jesus address Mary Magdalene merely as 'woman' (also simply *gunai*) at John 20:15.

At Mark 9:24, for the words 'help my unbelief', the NIV has 'help me overcome my unbelief'. The words 'me overcome' are, of course, interpretive and, if they must be included, should be in brackets. Surely the NIV translators have done the reader a disservice by offering their narrow interpretive opinion here. Matthew Henry clearly saw more in the passage than the NIV translators did: '*Help mine unbelief*, help me to a pardon for it, help me with power against it; help out what is wanting in my faith with thy grace, the strength of which is perfected in our weakness.'[1] Had the NIV translators used italics or brackets, at least their interpretive opinion would have been labelled clearly so that the unsuspecting reader would not confuse it with the words of the original text.

At John 10:36 the NIV has 'set apart as his very own' for *hegiasen*, which literally means 'sanctified' or 'set apart' or 'consecrated'. The words 'as his very own' have no equivalent in

[1]Henry, 5:510.

the original text. They are words of interpretation added by the translators. The interpretation, however, which has commended itself to most interpreters is that Jesus refers to being set apart for his sacred mission by his Father. Matthew Poole, for example, affirms that Jesus stated that he was 'set apart of God for the special work of man's redemption, and sent of God into the world with commission both to reveal and to do his will'.[1] The reader of the NIV, however, never has the privilege of considering this interpretation. The interpretive decision has been made for him by the translators; and by including their interpretive opinion without italics, they lead the uninformed reader to assume that the original text requires the words 'as his very own'.

Hebrews 13:4a has no verb. This has led scholars to debate whether the writer intended that his readers understand his words as a declaration or as an exhortation. Here the translator cannot remain neutral. He must either treat it as a declaration, as the KJV does ('Marriage *is* honourable in all, and the bed undefiled'), or as an exhortation, as the ASV does ('*Let* marriage *be* had in honor among all, and *let* the bed *be* undefiled'). Both the KJV and the ASV supply the proposed verbs in italics. The NIV, however, supplies verbs without brackets or italics ('Marriage should be honored by all, and the marriage bed kept pure'). Unlike with the KJV and the ASV, the reader of the NIV is given no indication that he is reading interpretation as well as text.

Concerning 1 Peter 4:6, Johnstone remarks, 'This verse is obscure, – judged, indeed, by many scholars to be as hard of interpretation as any statement found in Scripture . . . by some absolutely given up as a *locus desperatus*.'[2] Translators as a general rule have translated this verse literally; for example, the NKJV reads, 'For this reason the gospel was preached also to those who are dead.'[3] Perhaps more than with any other disputed passage, translators here have acted with caution. The NIV virtually stands alone in giving an interpretive translation: 'For this is the reason the gospel was preached even to those who are now dead.' At this

---

[1]Matthew Poole, *A Commentary on the Holy Bible* (reprint ed., Edinburgh: The Banner of Truth Trust, 1965), 3:335.

[2]Robert Johnstone, *The First Epistle of Peter* (reprint ed., Minneapolis: The James Family Christian Publishers, 1978), pp. 319–20.

[3]The KJV, ASV, RSV, NASB, NEB, and GNB treat the key word *nekrois* the same way (i.e., 'to the dead' or 'to those who are dead').

place, the note in *The NIV Study Bible* states, 'The word "now" does not occur in the Greek, but it is necessary to make it clear that the preaching was done not after these people had died, but while they were still alive.'[1] This interpretation is perhaps the correct one, but it is not by any means the only one. In any case, when translating such a difficult passage (a *locus desperatus*), the NIV at least should have put the word 'now' in italics or brackets.

3. THE OMISSION OF WORDS IN TRANSLATION

It is very rare in the work of translating for formal equivalence translators to omit words given by inspiration. Dynamic equivalence translators, however, frequently treat conjunctions, particles, pronouns, articles, adjectives, adverbs, and even phrases as surplus verbiage. Note the following examples from the NIV New Testament.

What has become of 'as' (*kathōs*) at Mark 1:2? What about 'since' (*epeidēper*) at Luke 1:1? What happened to 'of the house' (*oikou*) at Matthew 10:6? What became of 'unto himself' (*eis auton*) at Ephesians 1:5 or 'his' (*autou*) at Colossians 1:26?

The NIV translators take great liberty in omitting conjunctions and other transitional markers. Note, as one example, their treatment of the account of the faith of the Canaanite woman in Matthew 15:21–28. At 15:21 *kai* ('and' or 'then') is untranslated, although it is translated at 15:28. What has become of *kai idou* ('and behold') at 15:22? The conjunction *de* ('but' or 'then') is untranslated five times (*15:23, 24, 25, 26, 27*). This type of thing is characteristic of the NIV.

One marvels at the NIV's widespread elimination of one of Mark's most distinctive literary features – the repetitive use of the conjunction 'and' (*kai*) to introduce clauses and sentences, especially in narrative sections. And why is *euthus* ('immediately' or 'straightway'), another important Markan term, not translated at Mark 1:21, 30; 2:12; 3:6; 8:10? And what warrant can be pleaded for the widespread elimination of *idou* ('lo' or 'behold')? For example, of the sixty-two occurrences of *idou* in the Gospel of Matthew, the NIV translators leave it untranslated thirty-seven

[1] *The NIV Study Bible*, p. 1894.

times. Surely this kind of thing is without warrant by any just standard of translation.[1]

4. THE EROSION OF THE BIBLE'S TECHNICAL TERMINOLOGY

Supposedly in the interests of greater clarity, dynamic equivalence translators frequently eliminate the difficult or technical terms often found in the formal equivalence translations. It is asserted that we must translate so that the uninformed may read without encountering such strange terms or words. Often the charge is made as well that we cling to such technical words out of sentimentality or familiarity but not out of necessity.

In response we must ask, Was the Bible written without technical terms? Are rare and difficult words lacking in the original? If God inspired the original writers to use such terms, are we to be more fastidious than God? Do we have more concern for clarity than He does? If the Bible contains rare and technical words, why are they forbidden to the translator? Like any other discipline or field of study which has a unique or specialized message, the Christian faith has a technical vocabulary. These words communicate with precision; and their elimination, with the intent of communicating in 'everyday language' (undoubtedly a noble desire), generally tends to lesser precision.

At several points in the NIV there has been an erosion of the New Testament's technical vocabulary, apparently in the interest of simplicity of expression. In some cases the substitution of new terminology is limited to only some occurrences of a term. For example, why does the NIV render *dikaioō* everywhere with the familiar 'justify', except at Romans 2:13 and 3:20 where it reads

---

[1]'Faithful translation requires different stylistic levels: to a real extent it must reflect the character of the original. When the original is beautiful, its beauty must shine through the translation; when it is stylistically ordinary, this must be apparent.' *The Story of the New International Version*, p. 13. Calvin Linton observes: 'If any book requires careful attention to style when it is translated, it surely is the Bible. It is the self-revelation of God himself, through his own words and through those of his prophets, each of whom in turn is *animated* for the reader by his own style.' Calvin D. Linton, 'The Importance of Literary Style in Bible Translation Today', in *The NIV: The Making of a Contemporary Translation*, p. 15. Considering that these statements were written in defence of the NIV, does what the NIV's defenders say agree with what the NIV's translators have done in the examples noted above?

'declared righteous'?[1] No rationale is given for this, not even in the notes of *The NIV Study Bible*. Why is *huiothesia* translated as 'adoption as sons' at Romans 8:23 and 9:4 and as 'to be adopted as sons' at Ephesians 1:5, while no mention of adoption is found at Romans 8:15 ('sonship') or at Galatians 4:5 ('the full rights of sons')? Why is the term *mustērion* translated at most places with the familiar 'mystery', while at Matthew 13:11; Mark 4:11; Luke 8:10; and 1 Corinthians 2:7 the NIV has 'secret[s]', at 1 Corinthians 4:1 'secret things', at 2 Thessalonians 2:7 'secret power', and at 1 Timothy 3:9 'deep truths'?

In other cases there appears to have been a systematic attempt to replace the familiar (and more accurate) translation of certain terms. For example, the rather indefinite 'sacrifice of atonement' or 'atoning sacrifice' has been substituted for 'propitiation' at Romans 3:25 (*hilastērion*) and at 1 John 2:2; 4:10 (*hilasmos*).[2] *The NIV Study Bible* is to be commended \for explaining the NIV's rendering in terms of propitiation; however, there seems to be no good reason for giving an indefinite rendering in the text itself. Any translation that erodes a familiarity with the concept of 'propitiation' is to be lamented. Needless to say, it will be a sad day if large segments of the church lose the term 'propitiation' or cease to understand the important concept that it embodies.[3]

In recent days I have engaged in a study of the theme of local church unity. In surveying the biblical materials on the subject, I was struck with the importance that the term *homothumadon* ('with one accord') has in Luke's description of the unity of the church at Jerusalem. Of the twelve occurrences of the term in the New

[1] Justification, of course, involves more than the mere declaration of righteousness. Fundamentally it involves the imputation of our sin to Christ and the imputation of Christ's righteousness to us.

[2] See the excellent treatment of the subject of propitiation in Leon Morris, *The Apostolic Preaching of the Cross* (3rd ed., Grand Rapids: Wm. B. Eerdmans, 1965), pp. 144–213.

[3] John Murray notes that the concept of propitiation is intimately bound up with the doctrine of substitutionary atonement. 'To glory in the cross is to glory in Christ as the propitiatory sacrifice once offered, as the abiding propitiatory, and as the one who embodies in himself for ever all the propitiatory efficacy of the propitiation once for all accomplished.' John Murray, *Redemption Accomplished and Applied* (Edinburgh: The Banner of Truth Trust, 1979), p. 33.

Testament,[1] eleven are in Acts; the other occurrence is at Romans 15:6.

In the Pauline epistles, local church unity is likened to the harmony of parts in a human body; the point being that though there is great diversity in its members, there is an overarching vital unity in which each member is to display a body-mindedness, i.e., a personal and individual concern for the well-being of the body as a whole (cf. *Romans 12:4–5; 1 Corinthians 12:12, 24–27*). Thus in writing to the churches, Paul exhorts the members in terms drawn from the imagery of a body, that is, he exhorts them to be one in spirit, soul, heart, mind, and voice (cf. *Philippians 1:27–30; 2:2; Romans 15:5–6; 1 Corinthians 1:10*). In essence, Paul tells us that the local church is to be a body animated by one spirit, having one soul; and its members are to have hearts which beat together as one, minds which share the same convictions and perspectives, and mouths which speak with one voice.

When Luke describes the unity of the church at Jerusalem, he uses the adverb *homothumadon*, translated consistently in the ASV as 'with one accord'. The word is derived from *homos*, which means 'one and the same', and *thumos*, which can be variously understood as 'soul', 'heart', 'mind', 'will', or 'purpose'. The basic idea of *homothumadon* is 'unanimously'.[2] This is how Luke uses it with reference to the unity of the church at Jerusalem (*Acts 1:14; 2:1 [Byz]; 2:46; 4:24; 5:12; 15:25*); and this is the basic meaning in Luke's other uses of the word as well (*Acts 7:57; 8:6; 12:20; 18:12; 19:29*). This is also the sense in which Paul uses the term at Romans 15:6.

The compound word *homothumadon* is to be distinguished from the simple adverb *homou*, which merely means 'together'. In five of the occurrences of the term, however, the NIV translates *homothumadon* as if it were the simple adverb *homou* (*Acts 1:14*;

---

[1]Including the reading of the Byzantine text at Acts 2:1.

[2]Heidland correctly notes, 'In the NT *homothumadon* is used to stress the inner unanimity of the community. . . . *homothumadon* is here almost a fixed term in the vocabulary of the community.' *Theological Dictionary of the New Testament*, s.v. *homothumadon*, 5:186. See also James Hope Moulton and George Milligan, *The Vocabulary of the Greek Testament* (reprint ed., London: Hodder and Stoughton, 1963), p. 448. Although it is not used in the New Testament, the adjective *homothumos* means 'unanimous'.

2:46; 4:24; 5:12; 12:20).[1] At two places, the NIV translators render *homothumadon* merely as 'all' (*Acts 7:57; 8:6*). At the other places, they come nearer the sense of the word with 'we all agreed' (*Acts 15:25*), 'made a united attack' (*Acts 18:12*), 'as one man' (*Acts 19:29*), 'with one heart' (*Romans 15:6*). Anyone reading solely the NIV will miss one of Luke's important emphases with reference to the life of the early church at Jerusalem, that is, that in spite of the many differences between its individual members, their life together as the church was lived 'with one accord'.

The term *sarx* ('flesh') expresses a very complex set of ideas in the New Testament. In some cases, for example, the term is equivalent to 'body' (e.g., *Acts 2:31; 2 Corinthians 4:11; Ephesians 5:29*); in other cases the term expresses the idea of 'men' or 'people' (e.g., *Matthew 24:22; Luke 3:6; John 17:2*); in other passages the term is associated with the idea of human descent (e.g., *Romans 9:3, 5, 8; 11:14; 1 Corinthians 10:18*); in still other cases the term has a distinctly ethical importance (e.g., *Romans 7:5, 18, 25; 8:3, 4, 5, 8, 9, 12, 13*).[2] With some minor exceptions the formal equivalence translations consistently have used the English word 'flesh' to translate *sarx* and have left the reader to decide for himself what nuance of meaning to assign to the term in any given context. In most cases this has caused no problems for the reader, since the context has made it evident how 'flesh' was to be understood.[3]

At a number of places, especially in Paul's letters, where the term has a distinctly ethical significance, the NIV translates *sarx* as

[1] Excluding Acts 2:1, where there is a variant reading, with the Byzantine text reading *homothumadon* (with one accord) and the other major witnesses reading *homou* (together). Because of the way that the NIV treats *homothumadon* at other places in Acts, it is impossible to determine which reading it follows at 2:1.

[2] These four categories do not exhaust the list of ways that *sarx* is used in the New Testament. They are merely examples of usage. While I am convinced that in a number of places the NIV has missed the mark in its interpretive replacements for the translation 'flesh', the wide range of ways that *sarx* is rendered in the NIV is indeed an indication of the many nuances of meaning that the term has in the New Testament.

[3] I am not, of course, arguing that the same Greek word must always have the same translation in English. The context in which a word is used often determines the range of its meaning.

'sinful nature'.[1] Commenting on the NIV translators' choice of renderings, Wolf asserts:

In order to show that 'flesh' refers, not to the body, but to the sinfulness of man, the NIV has often rendered 'flesh' (*sarx*) as 'sinful nature' (cf. 'Rom. 8:3-5, 8-9'). While many readers would properly understand 'flesh' in the sense of 'human weakness', the translation 'sinful nature' avoids any misinterpretation of this key theological term.[2]

Wolf, of course, is correct in observing that *sarx* is a 'key theological term' which refers to the sinfulness of man. In describing man's sinfulness, however, Paul uses *sarx* in a very precise manner; and, indeed, we must be careful not to misinterpret the apostle's use of this important technical term. But what is Paul describing when he uses *sarx*?

When Paul uses *sarx* to describe man's sinfulness, he is not speaking of a distinct 'nature' in man but of a moral reality at work in man by virtue of the fall, i.e., indwelling sin. In unregenerate men, 'flesh' may be defined as 'reigning indwelling sin', so that to be 'in the flesh' is to be 'under the dominion of sin'. In the regenerate man, 'flesh' may be defined as 'remaining indwelling sin', so that although 'flesh' (indwelling sin) remains, it does not reign in the Christian.

This is how John Murray understood Paul's use of *sarx* in Romans. Commenting on Romans 7:5, on the phrase 'when we were in the flesh' (a reference to man in his unregenerate state), Murray observes:

'Flesh' in this ethically depreciatory sense means 'human nature as controlled and directed by sin'. . . . Hence when Paul speaks of having been 'in the flesh' he is referring to that period when sin exercised the dominion and is equivalent to saying 'when we were in sin'.[3]

---

[1]See, for example, Romans 7:5, 18, 25; 8:3, 4, 5, 8, 9, 12, 13; 13:14; 1 Corinthians 5:5; Galatians 5:13, 16, 17, 19, 24; 6:8; Ephesians 2:3; Colossians 2:11, 13.

[2]Herbert M. Wolf, 'When "Literal" is Not Accurate', in *The NIV: The Making of a Contemporary Translation*, p. 130.

[3]John Murray, *The Epistle to the Romans*, in *The New International Commentary on the New Testament* (reprint ed., Grand Rapids: Wm. B. Eerdmans, 1975), 1:244-45. Commenting on Romans 8:3, Murray says, 'The flesh is sinful human nature' (1:279). And commenting on Romans 8:5-8, Murray notes that the flesh is 'human nature as corrupted, directed, and controlled by sin' (1:284-85). This, of course, is not the same as saying that flesh is a distinct 'sinful nature' *per se*.

But commenting on Romans 7:14–25 (where Paul speaks of his experience as a regenerate man), Murray states, 'The tension which appears in 7:14–25 between that which Paul delights in, loves, approves, and wills and that which he is and does in contravention is inevitable in a *regenerate man* as long as *sin remains in him*'.[1] Speaking more specifically of verse 25, Murray says, 'The thanksgiving of verse 25 is not the language of the unregenerate man under the bondage of sin'.[2] Thus when Murray says that at 7:25 the flesh 'must be identified with the indwelling sin (17, 20)', he understands *sarx* differently than he did at 7:5.[3] At 7:5 *sarx* is reigning sin in the unregenerate; at 7:25 it is remaining sin in the regenerate.

A further issue which needs to be raised is the relation of *sarx* (as used ethically) and the human body. The fact that the word *sarx* in one context means 'indwelling sin' while in another context it means 'body' should at least dispose us to expect some relationship between the two. Some rightly are concerned to guard against the idea that matter is evil; but at the same time they are in danger of missing an important emphasis in Paul's teaching. What Paul calls 'the works of the flesh [*sarx*]' at Galatians 5:19–21, he calls 'the deeds of the body [*sōma*]' at Romans 8:13. Commenting on Romans 8:13, John Owen notes a relationship between *sarx* and *sōma*:

> The body in the close of the verse is the same with the flesh in the beginning: 'If ye live after the flesh ye shall die; but if ye . . . mortify the deeds of the body,' – that is, of the flesh. . . . The body, then, here is taken for that corruption and depravity of our natures whereof the body, in a great part, is the seat and instrument, the very members of the body being made servants unto unrighteousness thereby, Rom. vi.19. It is indwelling sin, the corrupted flesh or lust, that is intended. . . . The 'body' here is the same with . . . the 'old man', and the 'body of sin', Rom. vi.6; or it may synecdochically express the whole person considered as corrupted, and the seat of lusts and distempered affections.[4]

While we certainly want to avoid the idea that matter is intrinsic-

---

[1]Ibid., 1:258. Italics mine.
[2]Ibid., 1:259.
[3]Ibid., 1:270.
[4]John Owen, *The Works of John Owen*, ed. William H. Goold, Vol. 6: *Of the Mortification of Sin in Believers* (reprint ed., Edinburgh: The Banner of Truth Trust, 1967), pp. 7–8.

ally evil, we must not miss the point that 'flesh' truly is a psycho-somatic concept, involving body as well as soul.

The reader may be wondering why I have gone to such lengths to define *sarx* in its use as an ethical technical term. Let us return to Wolf's rationale for the NIV's rendering 'sinful nature'. First, Wolf argued that the translation 'sinful nature' was chosen to show that *sarx* refers 'not to the body, but to the sinfulness of man'.[1] While I appreciate the motives behind that concern, we must likewise be careful that the reader not conclude that *sarx* and 'body' have no relation at all.

My second concern with the translation 'sinful nature', how-ever, is more significant. Wolf asserts that 'the translation "sinful nature" avoids any misinterpretation of this key theological term'.[2] But does it? Multitudes have been taught that the Bible teaches that 'flesh' in the experience of the regenerate man is a distinct and unchanged nature, i.e., that 'flesh' is a 'sinful nature' along side of a newly added redeemed nature. Dabney traced this to the so-called 'Plymouth theology' of J. N. Darby and his followers.[3]

Most in our day have encountered the 'Plymouth' view of the constitution of the regenerate man in the writings of C. I. Scofield, who asserted:

The Scriptures teach that every regenerate person is the possessor of two natures: one, received by natural birth, which is wholly and hopelessly bad; and a new nature, received through the new birth, which is the nature of God Himself, and therefore wholly good. . . . The believer, on the contrary, while still having his old nature, unchanged and unchangeable, has received a new nature which 'after God is created in righteousness and true holiness.' . . . The 7th [chapter] of Romans is a record of the conflict of regenerate man with his old self, and is, therefore, intensely personal. 'I would,' 'I do not,' 'I would not,' 'I do,' is the sad confession of defeat which finds an echo in so many Christian hearts. In the 8th chapter the conflict still goes on, but how blessedly *impersonal*! There is no agony, *for Paul is out of*

---

[1]Wolf, p. 130.
[2]Ibid.
[3]See Robert L. Dabney, 'Theology of the Plymouth Brethren', in *Discussions: Evangelical and Theological* (reprint ed., London: The Banner of Truth Trust, 1967), 1:189–99.

it; the conflict is now between 'flesh' – Saul of Tarsus – and the Holy Spirit. Paul is at peace and victorious.[1]

This perspective was perpetuated by *The Scofield Reference Bible* in its note on Romans 7:15. There Scofield said:

The apostle personifies the strife of the two natures in the believer, the old or Adamic nature, and the divine nature received through the new birth. . . . The 'I' which is Saul of Tarsus, and the 'I' which is Paul the apostle are at strife, and 'Paul' is in defeat. In Chapter 8 this strife is effectually taken up on the believer's behalf by the Holy Spirit . . . and Paul is victorious.[2]

The idea that the believer is not personally engaged in the battle with remaining sin (but is 'out of it') is grossly unbiblical and dangerous to the souls of all who embrace it. Dabney, taking these ideas to their proper conclusions, warned:

Hence the presence, and even flagrancy, of indwelling sin, need suggest no doubts whatever whether his [i.e., the professing believer's] faith is a living one. Who can fail to see that there is terrible danger here of carnal security in sin? The darker danger, only less probable than this other, is, that the professed believer shall be taught to deny his responsibility wholly for the sins committed by this 'old man', who is '*a real man*', with a 'separate will and energy' from the 'new man'. We know nothing in the antinomianism of the 'Fifth Monarchy Men' more alarming than this. The doctrine is positively false. . . . Hence (and this is the Bible view) if any professed believer has the 'old man' as strong and lively as ever, it is proof positive that the 'new man' has never entered at all; his faith is vain; he is yet in his sins.[3]

Sadly, Dabney's fears were not unwarranted. Wherever these views have entrenched themselves, they have bred antinomianism and carnal security. Sin is regarded not as an act of the essential self but rather as an act of the old 'sinful nature'. There is no sense

---

[1] C. I. Scofield, *Rightly Dividing the Word of Truth* (reprint ed., Fincastle, Virginia: Scripture Truth Book Company, n.d.), pp. 44–49. Italics mine.

[2] *The Scofield Reference Bible* (New York: Oxford University Press, 1909), p. 1200. Although there was expansion and slight modification of this note in *The New Scofield Reference Bible*, the basic elements of Scofield's view were carried over unchanged. It is the expanded note which is found in *The Oxford NIV Scofield Study Bible*.

[3] Dabney, 1:197–98.

trying to mortify the old sinful nature, since that old nature is 'unchangeable'. The essential self, the new redeemed man, is 'out of' the battle in any case; the Spirit is now responsible for waging war against sin. Moreover, since the 'new man' is going to heaven in any case, why worry about the old 'sinful nature'; its remaining vigour is no reason for doubt about the final destiny of the soul. In our day the world is overspread with these 'carnal Christians', blissfully secure in their sins. Well did Dabney predict that these ideas would 'foster a certain type of religious experience, from which all doubt and anxiety are eliminated'.[1]

I am not suggesting that the NIV translators deliberately were trying to promote these views with their rendering of *sarx*. Wolf undoubtedly is being straightforward and honest in saying that their motive was to avoid misinterpretation of this key term. But how will those who have drunk deeply at the 'Plymouth' well read the words 'sinful nature' as a translation for *sarx*? And with the publication of *The Oxford NIV Scofield Study Bible*, it is highly likely that the NIV's 'sinful nature' will be read in the light of Scofield's views.[2] Far from avoiding the misinterpretation of *sarx*, the NIV's translation 'sinful nature' probably will contribute to the perpetuation of a serious error in the churches.

As noted at the beginning of this section, much of the erosion of technical terms in Bible translation is traceable to a concern for simplicity of expression. But an obsession with simplicity is dangerous when it comes to Bible translation. We need to be careful lest simplicity of expression erode precision of meaning. Sheehan rightly has observed that 'the translator who sets out to sacrifice everything on the altar of simplicity will sacrifice accuracy in the process'.[3] In the same vein Weeks comments, 'I fear that the simple translation makes the Bible easy to understand at the expense of there being a lot less to understand, a lot less of that which forces the reader to stop and reevaluate his concepts and categories'.[4] Surely it

[1]Ibid., 1:189.

[2]At Romans 7:15–25, *The Oxford NIV Scofield Study Bible* has the paragraph heading 'The Strife of the Two Natures' and the expanded form of Scofield's note from *The New Scofield Reference Bible*.

[3]Sheehan, p. 25.

[4]Noel K. Weeks, 'Questions for Translators', in *The New Testament Student and Bible Translation*, p. 107. See also the helpful material on Bible translation in Noel Weeks, *The Sufficiency of Scripture* (Edinburgh: The Banner of Truth Trust, 1988), pp. 270–90.

is better to teach each new generation the meaning of the Bible's technical terms than to eliminate them and produce a generation of supposedly biblically literate people, who in reality are biblically and theologically illiterate from having suffered long-term exposure to inaccurate and imprecise versions of the Bible.

Far from rejoicing at the elimination of the technical vocabulary of the New Testament, we ought to lament that the technical 'currency of the faith' is being lost so rapidly in some quarters. These terms are part of the warp and the woof of the fabric of the great confessions, commentaries, and theological works which have been of such value to the church. If the next generation of Christians ceases to trade in the old (i.e., biblical) technical currency, how long will they continue to value the old standards? We would do well to give heed to Nigel Turner's warning:

The Church today is concerned about communicating with the contemporary world and especially about the need to speak in a new idiom. The language of the Church had better be the language of the NT. To proclaim the Gospel with new terminology is hazardous when much of the message and valuable overtones that are implicit in the NT might be lost forever.[1]

5. THE LEVELLING OF CULTURAL DISTINCTIVES

The formal equivalence translation permits the modern reader to identify himself as fully as possible with the original readers and to understand as much as he can of biblical customs, ways of thinking, and modes of expression. Dynamic equivalence translators, however, tend to engage in 'cultural levelling', that is, they tend to express biblical ideas in terms of modern customs, modern ways of thinking, and modern modes of expression. For example, according to formal equivalence principles, a phrase such as 'greet

---

[1]Nigel Turner, *Christian Words* (Nashville: Thomas Nelson Publishers, 1981), p. viii. In discussing the topic of religious language, de Waard and Nida distinguish between primary and secondary religious language: 'The content of the Scriptures is best described as "primary religious language". Since it deals with supernatural events for which there are no finite models and since it reflects transcendental experiences for which ordinary language seems to be so inadequate, it is not at all strange that this primary religious language is in certain respects rather different from ordinary discourse. . . . It is almost inevitable that in primary religious language new and unusual expressions become hallmarks of the new community of faith, so that there is a good deal of in-group vocabulary; for example, *I am that I am*, *thus saith the*

one another with a holy kiss' (*Romans 16:16*) would be rendered literally; whereas according to dynamic equivalence principles, a modern equivalent might be selected, such as Phillips's 'give one another a hearty handshake all around'.

The NIV translators have not engaged in cultural levelling to the same degree as the translators of some other versions;[1] however, there are a number of places where it has occurred. For example, at 1 Peter 1:13 'girding up the loins of your mind' is rendered by 'prepare your minds for action'. In a similar vein, at Luke 12:35 the NIV has 'be dressed ready for service' for 'let your loins be girded about'. This is a very interesting example, because just two verses later the translators are content to retain the biblical culture's 'recline at the table' while substituting 'he will dress himself to serve' for 'he shall gird himself'. At least at this place, the application of cultural levelling appears to be somewhat arbitrary.

Lord, *the glory of the Lord*, *in the heavenlies*, *in Christ*, *emptied himself*, *became flesh*, and *saved by his blood*. . . . In contrast with primary religious language, derivative or secondary religious language is often quite different. In the first place, it tends to be explanatory and exegetical rather than kerygmatic. . . . As valuable as secondary religious language may be, it is not the language to be employed in the translation of the Scriptures. To do justice to primary religious language, one must preserve in translating something of the transcendent quality of the forms. It would be wrong to eliminate all of the "sublime obscurity" and try to rewrite primary religious language in the style of a textbook on biblical theology. Overzealous attempts to explain everything in the Scriptures may actually rob the primary religious language of its creative power to effect commitment and reorient human lives'. De Waard and Nida, pp. 21–23. At another place, de Waard and Nida note that 'there are certain important religious symbols which, though often obscure in their meaning, are necessarily important for the preservation of the integrity and unity of the biblical message'. Ibid., p. 38.

[1] The NIV translators claim to be philosophically opposed to cultural levelling in translation. 'Again, the Bible teems with figures of speech and other literary devices. Idioms abound, particularly in the Old Testament. The Hebrew text speaks of "the arm of the Lord", "the eyes of the Lord", and of his "mouth" and even of his "feet". Are these and similar expressions like them to be put into contemporary equivalents that will obscure their vigor? Or should translators find ways, consistent with good English, to retain enough of them to convey a sense of how the Hebrew writers thought and wrote? This is what the NIV tries to do, and in this respect it stands within the great tradition of Bible translation.' *The Story of the New International Version*, p. 13.

At Galatians 1:16 'flesh and blood' now is 'any man'. At Galatians 4:1 'though he is lord of all' has become 'although he owns the whole estate'. At Ephesians 2:2 'the sons of disobedience' are now 'those who are disobedient' (yet at 1 Thessalonians 5:5 'sons of the light and sons of the day' is retained). At Ephesians 2:3 'children of wrath' are now 'objects of wrath'. At Ephesians 3:5 'the sons of men' are now merely 'men'. At Romans 2:9 'every soul of man' has become 'every human being'.

It is commonly alleged that formal equivalence translations are 'culturally distant' from the modern reader, that today's reader has difficulty relating to the strange cultures of Bible times; thus, what is needed is a translation which is 'culturally relevant' to the modern Bible reader. The alleged cultural problem, however, causes less difficulty than is often suggested, not only because 'all people recognize that other peoples behave differently from themselves',[1] but also because of the large influence that the Bible has had on the development of English-speaking Western culture. Our language is suffused with biblical terms (justify, repent, grace, sin, revelation, conversion, etc.) and our culture has developed to a large degree under the influence of a biblical world view (although sadly this influence is eroding rapidly).

[1] Nida, *Toward a Science of Translating*, p. 168.

❧ 5 ❧

Dynamic Elements in the NIV
New Testament (2)

6. THE PRESENTATION OF THE INTERPRETATION OF
SCRIPTURE AS SCRIPTURE

All translation involves interpretation. Interpretation, of course, involves the influence of theology; and as all translation involves interpretation, so all translation involves theology. The idea of completely non-interpretive translation is a mirage chased only by those who have never engaged in the work of translation. Translators cannot avoid totally the necessity of making the interpretive decisions, nor can they avoid completely the influence of personal views of truth on their work. Translation is not hermeneutically neutral and translators are not theologically neutral.

All translators to some extent must make decisions which involve interpretation of the original (e.g., the selection of word equivalents, the translation of such things as verb tenses and participles and prepositions, the relation of clauses within a sentence, etc.). For example, at Ephesians 1:4 the prepositional phrase 'in love' may be taken with what precedes (as in the ASV) or with what follows (as in the NASB). The original text is grammatically ambiguous; and yet the translator cannot have it both ways. He must align 'in love' either with what precedes or with what follows. In this case an interpretive decision is unavoidable, even in the strictest formal equivalence translation.[1]

[1]There are, of course, many places where the translator is not forced to sort out a grammatically ambiguous text. He may choose to pass on the grammatical ambiguity to the reader. For example, at Romans 16:25 the

As a further example, look at Galatians 5:25. The translator must decide whether the two occurrences of *pneumati* should be translated as instrumental of agency (as in the ASV – 'If we live *by the Spirit, by the Spirit* let us also walk') or as locative of sphere (as in the NKJV – 'If we live *in the Spirit*, let us also walk *in the Spirit*'). Or should we treat each occurrence differently, like the NIV's 'Since we live *by the Spirit* [instrumental of agency], let us keep in step *with the Spirit* [instrumental of association]'. Each of these treatments of *pneumati* is grammatically possible and each gives a good sense to the passage; however, the translator must decide between them, and his decision must be made predominantly on theological and not on grammatical grounds (because the grammar is ambiguous). And, in the last analysis, his decision will be based on personal theological conviction, or, in the case of a committee translation, on the basis of corporate theological consensus.

This type of interpretive activity is not at all my concern in criticizing dynamic equivalence translations. Where the grammar is ambiguous or where it is capable of being literally translated in a variety of ways, in most cases the translator must make as much a theological as a grammatical decision. There are many places where this kind of interpretive interaction with the original text is unavoidable; and every translator, regardless of his commitment to a particular translation philosophy understands this.

This does not mean, however, that all translations are equally interpretive. Generally speaking, the formal equivalence translator intrudes his interpretive opinions only where the necessity of making grammatical decisions forces him to do so. By comparison, the dynamic equivalence translator tends to be relatively unrestrained in his theologizing. What the formal equivalence translator generally does only as a matter of necessity, the dynamic equivalence translator often does as a matter of choice.

The result is that with dynamic equivalence translations the

---

words *to kērugma Iēsou Christou* can be taken as a subjective genitive (i.e., that which Jesus Christ preached) or as an objective genitive (i.e., the preaching which is about Jesus Christ). The majority of translations pass the decision along to the reader with 'the preaching [or: proclamation] of Jesus Christ'. Among the major English versions, only the GNB departs from this procedure, rendering the words as an objective genitive ('according to the Good News I preach about Jesus Christ').

interpretive layer between the reader and the original text tends to be thicker than with formal equivalence translations. This follows naturally, of course, from the basic premise of dynamic equivalence translating. The more that the concern of the translator shifts from formal linguistic correspondence between text and translation to producing 'equivalent effect' in the mind of the modern reader, the more necessarily interpretive translation becomes. As Nida acknowledges, 'The translator is often inclined to be more interpretive on the basis of such a formula [i.e., dynamic equivalence] than if he attempts to stay closer to the actual wording of the original.'[1]

Where a translator operating on dynamic principles interprets properly and selects an English equivalent which truly produces 'equivalent effect', the result is relatively safe; in the final analysis the reader has not been misled, although he never gets to consider the interpretive options and may not be able to discern how others have arrived at a differing position. Where the translator, however, errs in perceiving the 'idea' or 'thought' which the original writer intended to communicate, he misguides the reader by his interpretive blunder. Because the formal equivalence translator is concerned to stay as close as possible to the original text (including its very words and form), he is less likely to mislead the reader than the dynamic equivalence translator.

The dynamic equivalence translator genuinely is seeking to help his readers understand the Bible; and for this he is to be commended. At the same time, however, he reveals a lack of confidence that the modern Christian is able to interpret the Bible for himself. After hearing one of my lectures on Bible translation, a correspondent put it this way: 'You say that the people who use a formal equivalence translation have the option of interpretation. Most people, however, are incapable of interpreting and so need a scholar to interpret for them.' In a more scholarly way, but in a similar vein, de Waard and Nida state:

It is unfair to the original writer and to the receptors to reproduce as ambiguities all those passages which may be interpreted in more than one way. In the first place, the reader will almost inevitably acquire a wrong impression as to the intent or purpose of the biblical writer,

[1]Eugene Nida, *Bible Translating* (London: United Bible Societies, 1961), p. 12.

since it would seem to the reader that the biblical writer was not concerned with communicating a message but only with 'playing language games'. In the second place, the translator places a very heavy burden on the receptor to determine which of two or more meanings may be involved. The average reader is usually much less capable of making correct judgments about such alternative meanings than is the translator, who can make use of the best scholarly judgments on ambiguous passages. Accordingly, the translator should place in the text the best attested interpretation and provide in marginal notes the appropriate alternatives.[1]

A number of things must be said in response. In the first place, I believe that it is incorrect to argue that the reverent reader of a formal equivalence translation will suspect the biblical writers of 'playing language games' when he comes upon passages capable of more than one interpretation. In such cases historically the people of God have confessed their own ignorance and prayed for the illuminating influences of the Spirit to attend their reading of the Word, while seeking to resolve the ambiguities by comparing scripture with scripture; they have indicted themselves for their own ignorance, not the biblical writers for 'playing language games'.

In the second place, if applied universally, the suggestion that 'the translator should place in the text the best attested interpretation and provide in marginal notes the appropriate alternatives' places too much authority into the hands of the translator. If applied in a limited way (i.e., to those places where grammatical necessity demands it), the translator would be doing only what is necessary by putting the best attested[2] interpretation in the text and would be doing the reader a service by putting alternatives in marginal notes. Where the text is not grammatically ambiguous, but only theologically ambiguous, however, the translator takes too much on himself by substituting even a 'best attested'

---

[1] De Waard and Nida, p. 39. In an earlier work, however, Nida observed, 'At times the translator may be misled by his own paternalistic attitude into thinking that the potential receptors of his translation are so limited in understanding or experience that they must have his "built in" explanations.' *Toward a Science of Translating*, p. 155.

[2] I am not sure what de Waard and Nida mean by 'best attested'. As I am using the words, I mean that interpretation which is best in accord with the analogy of faith, i.e., the overall teaching of the Bible; so that the 'interpretation' is in harmony with the body of revealed truth as a whole and not at variance with any of its individual parts.

interpretation for a literal rendering of the words. In these cases he should give a literal translation in the text and relegate interpretive suggestions, if he ought to give them at all, to marginal notes.

In the third place, the attitude toward the average Christian reader of the Scriptures expressed both by my correspondent[1] and by de Waard and Nida[2] is alarming to one whose spiritual and historical affinity is with the Protestant Reformation. While I am not saying that those translators who manifest such an attitude have repudiated the Reformation, I am saying that they have either consciously or unconsciously retreated to some degree from one of the Reformation's cardinal doctrines.

At the Council of Trent, the Roman Catholic Church codified her position on the interpretation of the Scriptures. According to the Council, supreme authority rested in 'holy mother Church, whose it is to judge of the true sense and interpretation of the holy Scriptures'.[3] The reformers protested against this attitude vigorously. Hodge gives an able summary of the reformed doctrine:

> The Bible is a plain book. It is intelligible by the people. And they have the right, and are bound to read and interpret it for themselves; so that their faith may rest on the testimony of the Scriptures, and not on that of the Church. Such is the doctrine of the Protestants on this subject. . . .
>
> What Protestants deny on this subject is, that Christ has appointed any officer, or class of officers, in his Church to whose interpretation of the Scriptures the people are bound to submit as of final authority. What they affirm is that He has made it obligatory upon every man to search the Scriptures for himself, and determine on his own discretion what they require him to believe and to do.
>
> . . . The most obvious reasons in support of the right of private judgment are,
>
> 1. That the obligations to faith and obedience are personal. Every man is responsible for his religious faith and his moral conduct. He cannot transfer that responsibility to others; nor can others assume it in his stead. He must answer for himself; and if he must answer for

---

[1]'Most people, however, are incapable of interpreting and so need a scholar to interpret for them.'

[2]'The average reader is usually much less capable of making correct judgments about such alternative meanings than is the translator, who can make use of the best scholarly judgments on ambiguous passages.'

[3]Quoted by E. H. Klotsche, *The History of Christian Doctrine* (reprint ed., Grand Rapids: Baker Book House, 1979), p. 253.

himself, he must judge for himself. It will not avail him in the day of judgment to say that his parents or his Church taught him wrong. He should have listened to God, and obeyed Him rather than men.

2. The Scriptures are everywhere addressed to the people . . . . To them are directed these profound discussions of Christian doctrine, and these comprehensive expositions of Christian duty. They are everywhere assumed to be competent to understand what is written, and are everywhere required to believe and obey what thus came from the inspired messengers of Christ. They were not referred to any other authority from which they were to learn the true import of these inspired instructions. It is, therefore, not only to deprive the people of a divine right, to forbid the people to read and interpret the Scriptures for themselves; but it is also to interpose between them and God, and to prevent their hearing his voice, that they may listen to the words of men.[1]

Translators should not intrude their interpretive opinions in the work of translation except where grammatical necessity demands it. To do otherwise is to erode the right of the people of God to exercise private judgment in interpreting the Scriptures. The theologically ambiguous should be left theologically ambiguous; each man, in reading the Bible, should be able to face the text for himself. No translator should usurp that right from him. Admittedly, formal equivalence translations require more effort on the part of the reader – more prayer, more study, more investigation, more thought; however, it is the duty and the right of the Christian to search the Scriptures for himself.

Before focusing our thoughts on examples from the NIV, perhaps an example involving other translations will help to illustrate what we have been saying. A clear example of unwarranted interpretive liberty with the original text is to be seen in the various renderings of *kauchōmetha ep' elpidi tēs doxēs tou Theou* at Romans 5:2. The KJV, NKJV, ASV, NASB, and NIV closely follow the original with 'we rejoice in hope of the glory of God'. Other translations, however, interpret the idea of the passage in one specific direction, i.e., of 'sharing' God's glory. The RSV has 'we rejoice in our hope of sharing the glory of God' (the GNB has essentially the same). The NEB renders the passage as 'let us exult in the hope of the divine splendour that is to be ours'. Of course, it is far from certain that the 'sharing' idea exhausts the options in

---

[1]Charles Hodge, *Systematic Theology* (reprint ed., Grand Rapids: Wm. B. Eerdmans, 1975), 1:183–85.

interpretation; yet the RSV, GNB, and NEB translators assume that it does. In reality, their interpretive prejudices have so coloured their translation that the poor reader is left with no interpretive option but theirs. No longer can he ask, 'What is "the hope of the glory of God" about which Paul is speaking?' The only question that he is aware of is, 'What does it mean to "share" God's glory?' or 'What can it possibly mean that "divine splendour" is to be ours?'

In my study of the NIV New Testament, I have found that the translators very frequently have offered their interpretive opinions under the guise of translation. The following are a few examples of this phenomenon.[1]

1. At Matthew 6:22 the NIV reads 'if your eyes are good' for the literal 'if therefore your eye is single'. Passing over other inaccuracies in translation,[2] let us focus on the rendering of *haplous*. The term *haplous* occurs only here and in the parallel passage at Luke 11:34; thus we must look outside of the New Testament to determine its range of meaning. Several meanings are attested in other sources, e.g., 'single', 'simple', 'sincere', 'wholehearted', 'pure'. Trench argues: 'It would be quite impossible to improve on "single" . . . being as it is from *haploō* . . . that which is *spread out*, and thus without folds or wrinkles . . . . This notion of singleness, simplicity, absence of folds, which thus lies according to its etymology in *haplous*, is also predominant in its use.'[3] Although it is a popular rendering, the idea of 'sound' (RSV, NEB, GNB), 'healthy' (NASB margin), or 'good' (NIV, NKJV) has only questionable lexical attestation. While these translations represent a possible understanding of the term in question, they are not the best attested lexically nor do they enjoy universal support among commentators. Indeed, J. A. Alexander regards this kind of translation as misleading:

[1]Many other examples of interpretive paraphrase could be cited. If the reader desires to pursue this matter further, additional examples may be found at Acts 26:20; Romans 1:3; 2:17; 6:4; 8:10; 9:16; 12:17; 1 Corinthians 2:4; 5:5; 7:17; 11:19; 12:6; 15:31; Galatians 2:17; 3:3, 10; 4:21; Ephesians 1:23; 2:3; 4:2, 7, 17; 5:3, 16; Colossians 2:2; 3:14; 1 Timothy 1:8; 3:4; 2 Timothy 1:14; 2:4; Hebrews 2:11; 6:1; 7:16; 9:28; James 1:2, 20; 2:7; 3:18; 1 Peter 4:10; 1 John 2:16; Jude 19; Revelation 13:10; 14:12.

[2]The conjunction *oun* is untranslated; *ophthalmos* is singular ('eye') not plural ('eyes').

[3]Richard C. Trench, *Synonyms of the New Testament* (reprint ed., Grand Rapids: Wm. B. Eerdmans, 1975), p. 204.

Single, in the strict and proper sense as opposite to double or to manifold, [is] the only meaning justified by usage or the context. The sense of *sound* or *healthy*, given by some writers, is a mere conjectural deduction from the supposed meaning of the corresponding epithet [*ponēros*, verse 23], which . . . may denote either physical or moral evil, and must therefore, it is hastily concluded, when applied to a bodily organ, mean diseased, disordered, and the parallel [*haplous*] of course can only mean the opposite condition. But the true deduction is the inverse one, from the specific to the vague term. As the former [*haplous*] certainly means simple, single, the indefinite term evil [*ponēros*] means of course defective or diseased in this particular respect, i.e. double, mixed, confused. . . . The indefinite sense put upon the term [*haplous*] by some not only violates all usage and the laws of lexicography, but utterly obscures the connection, and affords a pretext for the charge of incoherence. If there is no allusion to simplicity or singleness of sight, but only to its sound or healthy state, the illustration loses all its point, and must be treated as a mere digression or interpolation. On the other hand, if *single* have its proper sense, and *evil* be interpreted according to it, the comparison is perfectly adapted to its purpose, namely, that of showing, by a physical analogy, the vast importance, nay, the absolute necessity, of such a single and exclusive trust and love to God as had been just before enjoined upon our Lord's disciples.[1]

If the idea of 'single' is not carried over in translation, then, as Alexander observes, we stand in danger of missing the point which the passage makes as an illustration of the necessity of single-minded devotion to the Lord and of trust in his providential care.

2. At John 1:16, instead of the literal 'of his fullness we all received, and grace for [or: instead of, upon] grace', the NIV reads 'from the fullness of his grace we have all received one blessing after another'.[2] The original text speaks of 'his [i.e., the incarnate Word's] fullness', not 'the fullness of his grace'. In its context the phrase 'his fullness' (*tou plērōmatos autou*) is to be understood in terms of the words of 1:14, where the truth is declared that the incarnate Word is 'full [*plērēs*] of grace and truth'. At the least we must say that 'his fullness' consists of more than 'the fullness of his grace'; indeed, 'his fullness' is a fullness 'of grace and truth' (cf. *1:17*).

[1]Joseph Addison Alexander, *The Gospel According to Matthew* (reprint ed., Grand Rapids: Baker Book House, 1980), p. 182.
[2]Here the NIV seems to follow the GNB throughout and is just as dynamic in its rendering of the verse.

Moreover, although a case can be made for understanding the phrase 'grace for grace' in the way that the NIV apparently does (i.e., one blessing of grace after another), two things need to be said. First, the NIV rendering is pure interpretive paraphrase with little formal linguistic correspondence to the original text. Second, historically there have been at least five other interpretations of 'grace for grace' which have been proposed and defended by serious commentators.[1] For the reader of the NIV, however, the decision has been made for him.

3. At John 6:27 the NIV has 'on him [i.e., the Son of Man] God the Father has placed his seal of approval' for the literal 'for him God the Father has sealed'. The NIV interprets 'has sealed' (*esphragisen*) as 'has placed a seal of approval on' (the GNB has 'mark of approval'). Not everyone, however, agrees that this is the proper interpretation. The NEB has 'God the Father has set the seal of his authority'. The Berkeley Version has 'God the Father has certified him'. It is also possible that the word means 'mark (with a seal) as a means of identification'.[2] Though related, these ideas are not the same as 'seal of approval'. Again, the interpretive decision has been made for the reader.

4. At John 14:30 the text literally reads 'he [i.e., the prince of this world] has nothing in me [i.e., Jesus]'. The NIV reads 'he has no hold on me'. What do the NIV translators intend for us to understand by this rendering? Are they interpreting Jesus as saying that Satan presently does not have him in his grasp or in his power? Ryle understood the words 'he has nothing in me' to mean not that 'the prince of this world has no hold on me' but that Jesus 'had nothing about Him that Satan could lay hold on'.[3] These, of course, are two different ideas. The consensus of interpretive opinion is with Ryle.[4] The literal rendering leaves room for the

---

[1] See J. C. Ryle, *Expository Thoughts on the Gospels*: John (3 vols., reprinted., Edinburgh, The Banner of Truth Trust, 1987), vol. 1 pp. 39–40.

[2] William F. Arndt and F. Wilbur Gingrich, *A Greek-English Lexicon of the New Testament*, s.v. *sphragizō*.

[3] Ryle, vol. 3, p. 103.

[4] To the same effect see, for example, Albert Barnes, David Brown, John Calvin, Matthew Henry, George Hutcheson, Leon Morris, and Matthew Poole in their comments on this passage. Also in agreement is the study note in *The NIV Study Bible* (p. 1626): 'Since Christ was sinless, Satan could have no hold on him.'

interpreter to do his work; the NIV rendering, however, essentially eliminates the majority opinion from consideration.

5. At Acts 17:34 the text reads literally 'but certain [or: some] men, clinging to him, believed'. The NIV has: 'a few men became followers of Paul and believed'. Our concern is the word *tines* (from *tis*), here translated 'few'. The word itself is an indefinite pronoun, meaning simply 'certain' or 'some'. Unless there is further evidence to help the reader decide, there is no indication from the word itself whether the number of things or persons expressed by *tis* is large or small; it is an 'indefinite' pronoun. Yet here the NIV translators give us the interpretive rendering 'few'. There is nothing in the text which requires this interpretation. Perhaps this translation has been influenced by the widespread but erroneous opinion that Paul's ministry at Athens was a failure. In any case, the NIV rendering is misleading.

6. At Romans 1:17, for the phrase 'from faith unto faith' (*ek pisteōs eis pistin*), the NIV has 'by faith from first to last'. John Murray comments: 'There is much difference of opinion as to the precise intent of this formula. It has been interpreted as referring to the advance from one degree of faith to another [Calvin] or as equivalent to "by faith alone" [Hodge] or as implying that the righteousness of God is by faith from beginning to end [Dodd]'.[1] This last view is the one adopted by the NIV. Murray himself argues that Paul's purpose is 'to accent the fact that not only does the righteousness of God bear savingly upon us *through faith* but also that it bears savingly upon *every one* who believes'.

'From faith' points to the truth that only 'by faith' are we the beneficiaries of this righteousness, and so it is a 'faith-righteousness' as truly as it is a 'God-righteousness'. 'To faith' underlines the truth that every believer is the beneficiary whatever his race or culture or the degree of his faith. Faith *always* carries with it the justifying righteousness of God.[2]

It is not my purpose to suggest the correct interpretation of this difficult passage. My only purpose is to note that the NIV translators unfortunately have narrowed the field for the reader. The question no longer is, What does Paul mean by 'from faith

[1]Murray, *The Epistle to the Romans*, 1:31.
[2]Ibid., 1:32. See also Professor Murray's comments in his Appendix B (1:363–74).

unto faith'? The NIV reader now can only ask, What does Paul mean when he says 'by faith from first to last'?

7. At Romans 8:3, instead of the literal 'condemned sin in the flesh' (*en tē sarki*), the NIV has 'condemned sin in sinful man'. The most generally received view, however, is that Paul speaks of God's condemning sin vicariously in the flesh of Christ. Murray affirms: 'In that same nature which in all others was sinful, in that very nature which in all others was dominated and directed by sin, in that nature assumed by the Son of God but free from sin, God condemned sin and overthrew its power. . . . The battle was joined and the triumph secured in that same flesh which in us is the seat and agent of sin.'[1] Most likely the NIV translators have misinterpreted Paul here; and by substituting their interpretation for a literal translation, they mislead the reader.

Interestingly, the study note on Romans 8:3 in *The NIV Study Bible* takes issue with the NIV text. Commenting on 'in sinful man' as a rendering for 'in the flesh' (which is the NIV text's marginal rendering), the study note reads:

See NIV text note; 'flesh' may refer either to man's flesh or to Christ's. If the latter, it states where God condemned sin, namely, in Christ's human (but not sinful) nature – the interpretation that seems more consistent with Paul's teaching.[2]

8. Our consideration of Romans 8:28 is complicated by the presence of a variation in the testimony of the Greek manuscripts. The NIV translators have chosen to follow a well-attested reading which translated literally would be, 'And we know that, to [or: for] those who love God, God works all things together for good.' The NIV renders the verse in this manner, 'And we know that in all things God works for the good of those who love him.'

There is quite a difference, of course, between 'God works all things together for good' and 'in all things God works for the good'. Paul in essence teaches that because of God's sovereign control (i.e., because of the direct intervention and rule of Him who works all things after the counsel of His own will), 'not one detail works ultimately for evil to the people of God; in the end

[1]Ibid., 1:282. To the same effect, for example, are the comments of C. E. B. Cranfield, Charles Hodge, Robert Haldane, William Hendriksen, Matthew Henry, Matthew Poole, W. G. T. Shedd, and C. J. Vaughan.
[2]*The NIV Study Bible*, p. 1716.

only good will be their lot'.[1] In other words, Romans 8:28 is a definitive statement that God will work good. The NIV's rendering may be read to mean that God will in every circumstance exert his influence for the good of his people; but it is not clear from the NIV's translation that good will always be the outcome of God's exertion. The literal translation is unequivocal; the NIV is subject to being misconstrued and misapplied. At best it is a very weak statement concerning God's sovereign providential working in the affairs of his universe and his people.

9. At 1 Corinthians 6:18 Paul states, 'Every sin which a man commits is outside the body'. As Ellicott notes, 'These somewhat difficult words have received many interpretations.'[2] The most common interpretation is that the apostle is stating a universal principle which, however, has one exception, the sin of fornication. If this interpretation is correct, then what Paul means is 'every other sin,' although he says categorically 'every sin'. This, of course, is the interpretation followed by the NIV when it renders the words, 'All other sins a man commits are outside his body'.

Other interpreters have been troubled by this approach and have wondered, if this is what Paul meant, why he did not simply say 'every other sin'. Some of these interpreters have taken up the suggestion that Paul is stating and then contradicting a moral attitude or slogan current in Corinthian society or in the Corinthian church. Moule, for example, calls this a 'Corinthian "libertine" slogan' to the effect that 'no sin can affect a man's true "body": physical lust cannot touch the secure "personality" of the initiated'.[3] This interpretation is virtually eliminated, however, by the addition of the word 'other' in the NIV.

Generally the 'libertine slogan' interpretation also involves treating the statement at 6:12 ('all things are lawful to me') and 6:13 ('foods for the belly and the belly for foods') in a similar fashion.[4] It is interesting to note that this is exactly how the NIV treats these verses, as is evident by the quotation marks which

---

[1]Murray, *The Epistle to the Romans*, 1:314.

[2]Charles J. Ellicott, *A Critical and Grammatical Commentary on St Paul's First Epistle to the Corinthians* (Andover: W. F. Draper, 1889), p. 122.

[3]C. F. D. Moule, *An Idiom-Book of New Testament Greek* (reprint ed., Cambridge: The University Press, 1971), pp. 196–97.

[4]See Richard N. Longenecker, *Paul: Apostle of Liberty* (reprint ed., Grand Rapids: Baker Book House, 1976), pp. 232–33.

surround the words. This is confirmed by the notes on these verses in *The NIV Study Bible*. Of special interest, however, is the fact that this same interpretation is proposed in the note on 6:18, although the NIV translation will not support it. That note reads, 'Or, since the word "other" does not occur in the Greek text, Paul may be quoting a Corinthian slogan (see note on v. 12), which he refutes in the second half of the verse.'[1]

10. At 1 Corinthians 7:4 Paul states that 'it is good for a man not *to touch a woman*; but, because of fornications, let each man have his own wife and let each woman have her own husband.' The NIV translates the first clause as, 'It is good for a man not *to marry*.' The verb *haptō*, however, does not mean 'to marry' but 'to touch sexually'.[2] Although Paul uses the occasion to give extended instruction on the subject of marriage, the original written inquiry of the Corinthians (especially from what we know of the moral climate of Corinth, cf. 6:12–20) appears to have raised the question whether a celibate lifestyle (whether as a single person or as a married person) was to be the Christian ideal.[3] The NIV rendering misses this point. The NIV's marginal rendering is better, 'It is good for a man not to have sexual relations with a woman.'

11. At 1 Corinthians 7:4 a literal rendering of the text reads, 'The wife does not have power [or: authority] over her own body, but the husband; likewise also the husband does not have power [or: authority] over his own body, but the wife'. The NIV reads: 'The wife's body does not belong to her alone but also to her husband. In the same way, the husband's body does not belong to him alone but also to his wife.'

In the original text, the statement is categorical in nature and has been understood by many interpreters to mean that under normal circumstances the conjugal right within marriage is absolute, so

---

[1] *The NIV Study Bible*, p. 1741.

[2] See Ellicott, p. 125; Arndt and Gingrich, s.v. *haptō*; also *The New International Dictionary of New Testament Theology*, s.v. 'touch'. This is the meaning of the term in the LXX at Genesis 20:4, 6; Ruth 2:9; and Proverbs 6:29. The translation 'to marry' is unattested in the standard Greek lexicons.

[3] That is, the Corinthians were not asking, 'Should we be single or married?' but 'Should we be celibate, whether single or married?' Paul replied (1) that a life of celibate singleness is good, but not for everyone (7:2, 7–9), and (2) that married persons have sexual obligations to their partners (7:3–4), and therefore should engage in periods of celibacy only within strictly defined limits (7:5–6).

that 'neither has the right to refuse intercourse with the other' and that submission to one's marriage partner is a matter of debt (cf., *opheilē* at 7:3).[1] The NIV rendering, however, especially by the unwarranted addition of the word 'alone', speaks not in terms of absolute authority but in terms of shared authority. But if this is the apostle's meaning, then what is the significance of his stipulation in 7:5 requiring mutual consent before one may abstain from conjugal relations for a period of time in order to devote oneself to prayer? If the requirement of mutual consent is always of the essence of conjugal rights in marriage, if the 'power' or 'authority' is always shared, then one could veto one's marriage partner's conjugal rights regardless of the specific reason for doing so. If one votes 'yes' and the other votes 'no', the answer is 'no'. But if this is what Paul means, why is mutual consent needed for prayer? Why is the veto enjoyed at other times now invalid? Could not the 'praying' partner, as at other times, simply say 'no', regardless of the desire of the other partner?

The NIV rendering creates as many problems as it supposedly solves. It is better to translate literally and to leave it to the good sense of God's people to interpret scripture with scripture (e.g., *Matthew 7:12*) and to moderate the exercise of their absolute conjugal authority over their mates with such graces as self-denial and sensitivity and considerateness.

12. Paul's directive at 1 Corinthians 7:36 has been subjected to varying interpretations, especially with reference to the identity of the person designated by the word *parthenos*.[2] Literally the word means 'virgin' and this is how the KJV renders it. The ASV translators, however, understood Paul to be speaking of a 'virgin

---

[1]Geoffrey B. Wilson, *1 Corinthians: A Digest of Reformed Comment* (Edinburgh: The Banner of Truth Trust, 1978), p. 100. Ellicott (p. 126) states, 'Each must render the *opheilē* when the other asks for it.' Findlay states that '*she* is as much the mistress of his person, as *he* the master of hers'; and quotes with favour Bengel's observation that 'his (her) own is not his (her) own'. G. G. Findlay, *St Paul's First Epistle to the Corinthians*, in *The Expositor's Greek Testament* (reprint ed., Grand Rapids: Wm. B. Eerdmans, 1974), 2:823. At 7:3 the KJV rendering of *opheilē* ('benevolence') can be misleading in our day. Conjugal submission is not the granting of a favour but the paying of a debt.

[2]See the helpful summary in C. K. Barrett, *The First Epistle to the Corinthians*, in *Harper's New Testament Commentaries* (New York: Harper & Row, Publishers, 1968), pp. 182–84.

daughter' (with 'daughter' in italics).The NEB has 'partner in celibacy' (in a similar vein, Moffatt has 'the maid who is his spiritual bride'). The RSV has 'his betrothed'. Similar to the RSV, the NIV has 'the virgin he is engaged to'. The literal rendering is preferable; but if translators must offer their interpretations, they should at least use italics like the ASV. At the least the NIV should have 'he is engaged to' in italics or brackets.

13. Note the way *tēn huiothesian* at Galatians 4:5 is translated. The KJV, NKJV, ASV, NASB, and RSV stay with the standard lexical meaning, 'the adoption of [as] sons'. Several other translations, operating on dynamic principles at this place, though they retain the general idea of sonship, have eliminated the specific idea of adoption which is basic to the meaning of *huiothesia*.[1] The GNB has 'God's sons'. The NEB has 'the status of sons'. The NIV has 'the full rights of sons', with no hint as to how sonship was constituted. Why the NIV does this at this place (see also *Romans 8:15*) is a mystery, since at Romans 8:23, 9:4; and Ephesians 1:5 the NIV expresses the specific idea of 'adoption'. In any case, the liberty taken by the translators has impoverished the text.[2]

14. Scholars long have debated what Paul meant at Ephesians 4:9 when he spoke of Christ's descent 'into the lower parts of the earth'. Does Paul refer to a descent of Christ into Hell subsequent to his death? Or does he speak of Christ's death itself, his descent into the grave? Or is the reference to the incarnation of Christ, his descent from heaven to earth? The NIV translators seem to adhere to the last view, translating the phrase in question as 'to the lower, earthly regions'. The text is not grammatically ambiguous, only theologically unclear. Should not a literal rendering be given and the reader left to decide for himself?

15. At Colossians 1:25 Paul declares that according to the stewardship or commission given to him by God, he became a minister of the gospel and of the church for the sake of the Gentiles 'to fulfil the word of God'. Numerous interpretations have been made of the words 'to fulfil the word of God'.[3] The NIV adopts one

---

[1] See *Theological Dictionary of the New Testament*, s.v. *huiothesia*, 8:397–99.
[2] The study note in *The NIV Study Bible* (p. 1785) also recognizes the lack of accuracy of the NIV's translation.
[3] See the helpful treatment in John Eadie, *A Commentary on the Greek Text of the Epistle of Paul to the Colossians* (New York: Robert Carter and Brothers, 1856), pp. 93–95.

of them with its 'to present to you the word of God in its fullness'. In view of the context, however, the interpretation which the NIV promotes by its rendering misses the apostle's point. The 'word of God' in view is 'the mystery which has been hidden from the ages', that is, the inclusion of the Gentiles in the kingdom of God (*1:26– 27*; see also *Ephesians 3:2–11*). Paul's point is that God commissioned him to be the instrument of fulfilling God's promise to bless the Gentiles under the reign of the Messiah. Indeed, Paul's execution of his commission involves 'presenting [or: preaching] the word of God in its fullness', as is evident from the context; however, the point which Paul is making is broader than that. As the 'apostle to the Gentiles', Paul in his person and in his apostolic commission, as well as his message, is the fulfilment of the word of God.[1]

16. In Colossians 3:5 Paul exhorts his readers, 'Put to death therefore your members [*melē*, from *melos*] which are upon the earth: fornication, uncleanness, passion, evil desire, and covetousness, which is idolatry'. Instead of the literal 'your members which are upon the earth', the NIV has 'whatever belongs to your earthly nature'. In its attempt to clarify the apostle's figure of speech, however, the NIV has destroyed it. Here Paul uses metonymy, a figure of speech in which the name of one thing (the bodily members) is used of another thing associated with it (the sins of which the bodily members are the instruments).

Two passages in Romans help us to understand Paul's figure of speech here in Colossians 3:5. At Romans 7:23, Paul speaks of indwelling sin (cf. *7:20*) as a 'law in my members' and as 'the law of sin which is in my members'. At Romans 8:13, he speaks of putting to death 'the deeds of the body'. There is no question that in Colossians 3:5, as in Romans 7:23 and 8:13, Paul associates sin with the physical members of the body; and although he is not advocating a view that the physical body is inherently evil, we must not miss his point that the physical members of the body are involved intimately in man's sinning.[2]

[1] See also Romans 15:19, 'I have fulfilled [*me . . . peplērōkenai*] the gospel of Christ'.

[2] Commenting on Romans 7:23, Murray (*The Epistle to the Romans*, 1:267) observes: 'If the thought is focused on our physical members . . . we are not to suppose that "the law of sin" springs from or has its seat in the physical. It would merely indicate . . . that the apostle brings to the forefront the concrete and overt ways in which the law of sin expresses itself and that our physical members cannot be divorced from the operation of the law of sin.'

At Colossians 3:5, the NIV, with its 'whatever belongs to your earthly nature', obscures the apostle's point and destroys his figure of speech. Moreover, note that the NIV's translation of *melos* here is at variance with their translation of the term at Romans 7:23 ('the members of my body'). The reader who uses only the NIV would never suspect that there is a linguistic link between Romans 7:23 and Colossians 3:5.

17. The words *to heautou skeuos ktasthai* ('possess his own vessel') at 1 Thessalonians 4:4 have been interpreted in a variety of ways. Other than the article *to*, each word has been the subject of debate among commentators. Should *heautou* be treated as a true reflexive pronoun ('himself') or merely as a possessive pronoun ('his')? Does *skeuos*, which literally means 'vessel', here mean 'body' or 'wife'? Does the infinitive *ktasthai* (from *ktaomai*) mean 'possess' (KJV, ASV, NASB, NKJV) or 'acquire' ('take', RSV)?[1]

The preponderance of evidence appears to indicate that we should understand Paul as exhorting, in view of the danger of fornication and adultery, that a man should possess his wife (or acquire for himself a wife) in a holy and honourable manner. The NIV renders the clause as 'to control his own body'. But the verb *ktaomai* nowhere else is attested as having the meaning 'to control'; thus, the NIV rendering is greatly in doubt.[2] While a literal rendering such as 'to possess his vessel' leaves the reader room to decide the correct interpretation for himself, the NIV rendering, greatly in doubt to begin with, leaves the reader no latitude in interpretation.

18. At 1 Timothy 1:16, Paul declares that he received mercy as the 'first' of sinners in order that in him Christ might display 'all of his longsuffering' (or: 'the whole of his longsuffering') as a pattern

---

[1] On this passage, see the helpful discussion in John Eadie, *A Commentary on the Greek Text of the Epistle of Paul to the Thessalonians* (reprint ed., Minneapolis: James and Klock Christian Publishing Co., 1977), pp. 127–30; and Leon Morris, *The First and Second Epistles to the Thessalonians*, in *The New International Commentary on the New Testament* (Grand Rapids: Wm. B. Eerdmans, 1959), pp. 123–24.

[2] Moulton and Milligan (p. 362) propose that the verb means 'to master', yet they offer no corroborating evidence. Other than the NIV, among English translators only Conybeare (who clearly identifies his rendering as 'interpretation') concurs in that judgment. W. J. Conybeare and J. S. Howson, *The Life and Epistles of St Paul* (New York: Charles Scribner & Company, 1870), 1:394.

or prototype. He believed that in his case, the divine patience 'had been stretched to the uttermost'; and he 'regarded himself, so to speak, as a sort of thermometer or other means of measurement, which on the Damascus road registered the highest point'.[1]

The NIV renders the key phrase (*tēn hapasan makrothumian*) as 'his unlimited patience'.[2] The term *hapas*, however, nowhere has the sense of 'unlimited'; the word simply means 'all' or 'the whole'. Moreover, nowhere does the Bible teach that God's patience is unlimited; on the contrary, it has been argued quite cogently that of all of God's marvellous attributes, his patience is the only one which is not unlimited. That God's patience is not limitless is evident from the universal flood in the days of Noah, from the captivity of Israel in Babylon, from the destruction of Jerusalem in the first century A.D., and from the promise of the coming of the final Day of the Lord in conjunction with Christ's second advent.[3] Moreover, God demonstrates that his patience has limits every time that he takes the breath of life from unconverted men who have squandered away the opportunity to be reconciled to him through Christ. The NIV's rendering is unfortunate and potentially promotive of a very dangerous conception of God.

19. In Philemon 6 Paul prays for Philemon (in the literal rendering of the ASV) 'that the fellowship of thy faith may become effectual, in the knowledge of every good thing which is in you, unto Christ'. The NIV gives a very loose interpretive paraphrase: 'I pray that you may be active in sharing your faith, so that you will have a full understanding of every good thing we have in Christ.' This paraphrase undoubtedly will be misleading, especially to the modern evangelical reader, who will understand Paul as praying 'that you may be active in witnessing' (for 'sharing your faith' and 'witnessing' or 'giving your personal testimony' are synonymous terms in our day). But Paul does not have witnessing in mind at all. The subject is good deeds ('your faith and love') 'toward all the saints', that is, good deeds rooted in faith and love to Christ (see

[1] Ronald A. Ward, *Commentary on 1 and 2 Timothy and Titus* (Waco, Texas: Word Books, 1974), p. 38.

[2] The same as The Berkeley Version. The Twentieth Century New Testament has 'his exhaustless patience'.

[3] On the relationship of the Flood, the longsuffering of God, and the coming Day of the Lord, see 2 Peter 3:3–10. Those who presume on God's 'unlimited' patience are to learn the lesson of history displayed in the Flood.

verses 5 and 7). And, as is the case elsewhere in Paul's letters, his prayer here sets the stage for his exhortation, in this case his exhortation to Philemon concerning Onesimus (*dio*, 'therefore', verse 8).

20. At Hebrews 12:4 the writer declares to his readers, 'You have not yet resisted unto blood, striving against sin'. The NIV, with its 'you have not yet resisted to the point of shedding your blood',[1] takes these words to mean that although the original readers had suffered persecution and the loss of possessions (*10:32–34*), they had not yet actually had to shed their blood in martyrdom. This is a possible interpretation of the words; and, thus, the NIV may be correct in its interpretive paraphrase. But this is not the only interpretation of the writer's words; and, where this is the case, it seems better to translate literally and leave the reader latitude in interpretation.

It is possible that the language of Hebrews 12:4 is metaphorical and that it has to do with how Christians are to treat their remaining sin. In Hebrews, remaining sin is pictured as the formidable foe of perseverance, a foe who must be resisted at any cost. According to Hebrews 3:12–13, it is the deceitfulness of sin which, if left unchallenged and unmortified, will produce an evil heart of unbelief and apostasy. Thus, the professing Christian must be prepared to resist every proposal of indwelling sin as if in a life and death struggle. In order to run with perseverance the race set before us, we must lay aside 'the sin which so easily ensnares us' (*12:1*). The sluggish running of those to whom Hebrews was written indicated that perhaps for them mortification of sin and perseverance in the faith were not yet life and death issues. Otherwise, they would not have been so easily wearied in the way. Thus, using a striking metaphor, the writer warns them that in their striving against sin 'you have not yet resisted unto blood', that is, battling against sin has not yet become for you a life and death struggle.

21. At 1 Peter 3:7 the apostle instructs Christian husbands to dwell with their wives 'according to knowledge' (*kata gnōsin*). The NIV's rendering instructs husbands to 'be considerate as you live with your wives'. Now certainly considerateness is an important part of a husband's living with his wife 'according to knowledge';

[1] Like the RSV and the NEB. The GNB reads 'had to resist to the point of being killed'.

[59]

however, the NIV's rendering greatly narrows the concern of the apostle's exhortation. Considerateness is one manifestation of relating to one's wife 'according to knowledge', but it is not the sum total of what Peter had in mind. John Brown notes:

We rather think . . . that the meaning is, let him conduct himself intelligently, wisely, prudently. . . . The peace of the family, the comfort, and even the spiritual improvement both of the wife and of the husband, depend on this holy discretion. This knowledge, or wisdom, will enable them to form a just estimate of his wife's character, of her talents, her acquirements, her temper, her foibles, and will lead him to act accordingly. Christian husbands should act circumspectly, not as fools, but as wise.[1]

Note also the analysis of Alan Stibbs:

The Christian husband should let all his living together with his wife be informed and guided by a proper awareness of her condition in relation to himself both in nature and grace. On the one hand, naturally, he should recognize her more limited physical powers as a woman, and should give her corresponding consideration and protection. Only so will he render her due honour and be worthy of her marital confidence and devotion. On the other hand, spiritually, he should recognize their full equality as fellow-sharers in the grace of God, and in His gift to them both of eternal life. He should, therefore, live with her as a man fully aware that, in addition to the natural enjoyment of each other, they are, as Christians, called together to a spiritual fellowship with God and Christ, a sphere in which his wife is not weaker or inferior, but a joint-heir. Only if this delicately balanced fellowship between husband and wife is thus properly maintained will their union reach its true Christian fulfilment.[2]

And as helpful as the comments of Brown and Stibbs are, nevertheless, even they may not embrace all that the Spirit had in mind; how much less the narrow interpretive paraphrase of the NIV.

The NIV also frequently takes interpretive liberty with prepositional phrases. Numerous examples illustrate this widespread phenomenon. Unlike the preceding examples, however, in the

[1] John Brown, *Expository Discourses on 1 Peter* (reprint ed., Edinburgh: The Banner of Truth Trust, 1980), 1:569.
[2] Alan M. Stibbs, *The First Epistle General of Peter*, in *The Tyndale New Testament Commentaries* (reprint ed., Grand Rapids: Wm. B. Eerdmans, 1981), p. 127.

interest of not wearying the reader, I will not include an analysis of the examples. Following the biblical reference, two renderings will be given: (1) a literal, formal equivalence translation (designated as FET), usually that of the ASV, and (2) the interpretive paraphrase of the NIV.

Matt. 21:32	(FET) in the way of righteousness
	(NIV) to show you the way of righteousness
John 17:11	(FET) in your name
	(NIV) by the power of your name
Rom. 6:19	(FET) to iniquity unto iniquity
	(NIV) to ever-increasing wickedness
Rom. 7:5	(FET) in the flesh
	(NIV) controlled by the sinful nature
Rom. 10:4	(FET) unto righteousness
	(NIV) so that there may be righteousness
Rom. 15:5	(FET) according to Christ Jesus
	(NIV) as you follow Christ Jesus
Gal. 1:11	(FET) according to man
	(NIV) something that man made up
Gal. 3:18	(FET) is of the law
	(NIV) depends on the law
Gal. 4:29	(FET) after the flesh
	(NIV) in the ordinary way
Gal. 4:29	(FET) after the Spirit
	(NIV) by the power of the Spirit
Eph. 1:17	(FET) in the knowledge of him
	(NIV) so that you may know him better
Eph. 4:19	(FET) with greediness
	(NIV) with a continual lust for more
Phil. 2:1	(FET) in Christ
	(NIV) from being united with Christ
Col. 1:16	(FET) in truth
	(NIV) in all its truth
Col. 1:11	(FET) unto all patience and longsuffering
	(NIV) so that you may have great endurance and patience
Col. 1:29	(FET) according to his working
	(NIV) with all his energy

1 Thess. 4:2	(FET) through the Lord Jesus
	(NIV) by the authority of the Lord Jesus
1 Tim. 1:16	(FET) unto eternal life
	(NIV) and receive eternal life
1 Tim. 1:18	(FET) by them
	(NIV) by following them
1 Pet. 1:5	(FET) unto a salvation
	(NIV) until the coming of the salvation
1 Pet. 2:2	(FET) unto salvation
	(NIV) in your salvation
Jude 21	(FET) unto eternal life
	(NIV) to bring you to eternal life

As both classes of examples demonstrate, the NIV translators have not limited their interpretive activity to places where the original text is grammatically ambiguous. On the contrary, they have been too unrestrained in offering their interpretive opinions. Too often they have assumed the role of expositor; but the translator's task is not that of an expositor. His job is not to give a running commentary nor to explain the parts of the text that are theologically difficult to understand. A translator is not called upon to settle questions that have divided interpreters; and if he tries to do so, he takes too much on himself.

The translator's role is like that of an ambassador to a foreign people. He is to be faithful and precise in delivering the words which God has given to him. If this is his task, and it is, then only a careful formally equivalent rendering of the original will pass on to the people of God the message which the Lord intended us to receive.

7. THE PARAPHRASING OF THE BIBLICAL TEXT

The paraphrastic method of translation is one 'in which the translator restates the gist of the text in his own words'.[1] The formal equivalence method of translation is philosophically opposed to paraphrase; the dynamic equivalence method, however, has an affinity for it. Frequent paraphrase is a mark of a dynamic

[1]*The Story of the New International Version*, p. 12.

equivalence translation. Indeed, Price refers to the dynamic equivalence method as 'scientific paraphrase'.[1]

The Committee on Bible Translation claims that in the NIV there is only 'a minimum' of actual paraphrase.[2] But is this affirmation accurate? I do not think so; unless, of course, the term 'minimum' has ceased to mean 'the least amount attainable'.[3] In my comparison of the NIV New Testament with the Greek New Testament, I found that the NIV translators frequently engaged in paraphrase. Certainly, the level of paraphrase is not 'the least amount attainable'. The following examples will follow the pattern described above, i.e., (1) a literal rendering (again designated as FET) and (2) the NIV's paraphrase. I hope that the reader is not wearied by the number of examples; but it is necessary to establish that paraphrase is not an isolated phenomenon in the NIV New Testament.[4]

Matt. 1:25	(FET) he knew her not
	(NIV) he had no union with her
Matt. 2:10	(FET) they rejoiced with exceeding great joy
	(NIV) they were overjoyed
Matt. 6:14	(FET) if you forgive men their trespasses
	(NIV) if you forgive men when they sin against you
Matt. 8:25	(FET) we perish
	(NIV) we're going to drown

[1]Price, p. 27. Price (pp. 18–36) discusses the significant place that structural linguistics and transformational grammar have in the theory of dynamic equivalence. He argues (p. 37) that it is not the use but the misuse of transformational grammar which makes dynamic equivalence theory defective. With reference to paraphrase he concludes (p. 27): 'It is quite clear that paraphrase is unavoidable with dynamic equivalence theory. . . . This is primarily true because of the subjectivity involved in the transfer step. The failure to employ transfer rules, but rather to depend on the translator's subjective judgment, makes it almost certain that the information transferred to the receptor language will lack complete equivalence with the information of the source message. Thus the theory fails to accomplish equivalence; it is instead scientific paraphrase.'

[2]*The Story of the New International Version*, pp. 12–13.

[3]*The Oxford English Dictionary*, s.v. 'minimum'.

[4]Only a small fraction of the instances noted in my research are cited. In his own study of the NIV the reader will not have to search far to find additional examples.

Matt. 10:22	(FET)	for my name's sake
	(NIV)	because of me
Matt. 12:49	(FET)	and he stretched forth his hand towards his disciples and said
	(NIV)	pointing to his disciples, he said
Matt. 13:33	(FET)	in three measures of meal
	(NIV)	into a large amount of flour
Matt. 15:28	(FET)	let it be to you as you desire
	(NIV)	your request is granted
Matt. 22:16	(FET)	you are true
	(NIV)	you are a man of integrity
Matt. 23:3	(FET)	for they say, and do not
	(NIV)	for they do not practise what they preach
Matt. 25:21	(FET)	enter into the joy of your Lord
	(NIV)	come and share your master's happiness
Matt. 26:10	(FET)	she has worked a good work unto me
	(NIV)	she has done a beautiful thing to me
Matt. 26:25	(FET)	you have said
	(NIV)	yes, it is you
Mark 1:2	(FET)	before your face
	(NIV)	ahead of you
Mark 1:7	(FET)	and he preached, saying
	(NIV)	and this was his message
Mark 9:42	(FET)	offend (or: cause to stumble)
	(NIV)	sin
Luke 1:15	(FET)	from his mother's womb
	(NIV)	from birth
Luke 1:42	(FET)	the fruit of your womb
	(NIV)	the child you will bear
Luke 7:13	(FET)	he had compassion on her
	(NIV)	his heart went out to her
Luke 12:30	(FET)	the nations of the world
	(NIV)	the pagan world
Luke 12:50	(FET)	I have a baptism to be baptized with
	(NIV)	I have a baptism to undergo
John 1:20	(FET)	and he confessed and denied not; and he confessed
	(NIV)	he did not fail to confess, but confessed freely

John 2:16	(FET) make not my Father's house a house of merchandise
	(NIV) how dare you turn my Father's house into a market
John 3:6	(FET) that which is born of the flesh is flesh; and that which is born of the Spirit is spirit
	(NIV) Flesh gives birth to flesh, but the Spirit gives birth to spirit
John 4:50	(FET) the man believed the word that Jesus spoke to him
	(NIV) the man took Jesus at his word
John 5:30	(FET) I seek not my own will, but the will of him who sent me
	(NIV) I seek not to please myself but him who sent me
John 9:34	(FET) and do you teach us?
	(NIV) how dare you lecture us!
John 10:32	(FET) good works
	(NIV) great miracles
John 13:1	(FET) he loved them unto the end
	(NIV) he now showed them the full extent of his love
John 17:23	(FET) that they may be perfected into one
	(NIV) may they be brought to complete unity
Acts 1:4	(FET) the promise of the Father
	(NIV) the gift my Father promised
Acts 18:6	(FET) I am clean
	(NIV) I am clear of my responsibility
Rom. 2:17	(FET) boast in God
	(NIV) brag about your relationship to God
Rom. 3:20	(FET) the knowledge of sin
	(NIV) we become conscious of sin
Rom. 9:16	(FET) so then it is not of him that wills, nor him who runs, but of God who shows mercy
	(NIV) it does not, therefore, depend on man's desire or effort, but on God's mercy
Rom. 15:5	(FET) God . . . grant you to be of the same mind
	(NIV) God . . . give you a spirit of unity

1 Cor. 1:10	(FET)	that you all say the same thing
	(NIV)	that all of you agree with one another
1 Cor. 3:15	(FET)	yet so as through fire
	(NIV)	but only as one escaping through the flames
Gal. 1:16	(FET)	flesh and blood
	(NIV)	any man
Eph. 5:16	(FET)	redeeming the time
	(NIV)	making the most of every opportunity
Col. 1:9	(FET)	that you may be filled
	(NIV)	asking God to fill you
Col. 2:1	(FET)	not seen my face in the flesh
	(NIV)	not met me personally
Col. 2:11	(FET)	in putting off of the body of the flesh
	(NIV)	in the putting off of the sinful nature
1 Thess. 4:6	(FET)	the Lord is an avenger
	(NIV)	the Lord will punish
1 Tim. 5:17	(FET)	who labour in the word and teaching
	(NIV)	whose work is preaching and teaching
James 1:22	(FET)	be doers of the word and not hearers only, deceiving yourselves
	(NIV)	do not merely listen to the word, and so deceive yourselves. Do what it says.
James 5:11	(FET)	the end of the Lord
	(NIV)	what the Lord finally brought about
1 John 2:6	(FET)	he that says he abides in him ought himself also to walk as he walked
	(NIV)	whoever claims to live in him must walk as Jesus did

In the examples just cited, the interpretive intrusion of the translator is less serious (at least in my judgment) than the examples given in the preceding section. In some cases, the paraphrastic rendering does help make the text clear to the modern English reader. Yet, for all this, extensive paraphrase (such as we see in the NIV New Testament) greatly reduces a version's usefulness as a serious Bible study tool, especially for the reader who does not read Greek and Hebrew and who is thus dependent on the formal accuracy of the English translation that he is using as a study Bible.

In the preceding chapter and this one, we have examined the NIV in the light of seven characteristics of dynamic equivalence translations. In each category there was found significant affinity with the philosophy of dynamic equivalence. In fact, it is difficult to avoid the conclusion that the NIV translators have used the dynamic equivalence method to a large degree. The NIV Committee claims that they made a 'flexible use of concordance and equivalence'; this writer is persuaded that the NIV is oriented more in the direction of 'equivalence' (i.e., dynamic equivalence).

∽ 6 ∽

Is the NIV an Accurate Translation?

In the preceding two chapters, we saw that the NIV has been influenced heavily by the philosophy of dynamic equivalence. And although the NIV certainly is not as dynamic as the Good News Bible or the New English Bible, nevertheless, it has more in common with the dynamic equivalence versions than with the formal equivalence versions.

But is the NIV an accurate translation? Is the NIV accurate enough as a translation to warrant its becoming the standard version of the English-speaking world? Does the NIV meet the church's need for an accurate translation of the Scriptures, which are her only standard of faith and practice? Our answer to these questions depends, of course, on our definition of accuracy.

If we define accuracy of translation in terms of dynamic equivalence principles, virtually any rendering may be judged accurate; unless, of course, the consensus of opinion is that the translator has missed the 'idea' of the original author. If the translator divides complex sentences, adds or omits words, eliminates technical terms, makes the text modern culturally, injects his interpretive opinions, or engages in outright para- phrase, it is of no great concern. As long as he still gives his readers the general ideas of the original text, he is not guilty of inaccuracy in translation. By such a standard, of course, the NIV is an accurate translation. But if we define accuracy in terms of formal equivalence principles, that is, in terms of close correspondence to the structure and wording of the original texts, then the NIV must be judged inaccurate on a number of counts, as the preceding chapters demonstrate.

Which standard of accuracy should we use? I am convinced that we must view accuracy in terms of formal equivalence. I cannot conclude otherwise with a clear conscience. Since the inspiration of the Bible is both verbal and plenary (i.e., since inspiration extends to the very words of Scripture, and equally to all the words of Scripture), and not just dynamic (i.e., the error that inspiration has to do only with the 'ideas' or 'thoughts' of the Bible), then the accuracy of translations must be judged by principles which reflect a recognition of this most fundamental truth concerning the nature of the Scriptures. But is the dynamic equivalence philosophy of translation ultimately consistent with such a recognition? I do not believe that it is.

In the dynamic equivalence method of translation, the individual word is not the primary unit in translation. But, if the individual word is not the primary unit in translation, then it is hard to defend the premise that the individual word should be regarded as the primary unit in inspiration either. Indeed, if the individual word is abandoned as the primary unit of translation, what practical significance would a doctrine of the verbal-plenary inspiration of the originals have for the Bible reader who could not read the Greek and Hebrew texts?

In an earlier chapter, I asserted that the general tendency has been to find dynamic translation associated with heterodox views of biblical inspiration and authority. In all fairness, the NIV seems to be an exception to this tendency. Although the NIV has been influenced heavily by the dynamic equivalence philosophy of translation, its translators reportedly hold high views of biblical inspiration and authority. These reports are undoubtedly true; and I have no desire to cast a shadow on their reputation for orthodoxy. I am certain that their high view of the Scriptures and their love for the people of God were precisely what motivated their undertaking the NIV project. But I must assert, however, that in the final analysis such a heavy use of the dynamic equivalence philosophy is at odds with the doctrine of verbal-plenary inspiration.

Perhaps this generation of Bible translators will continue to embrace orthodox views of Scripture while using the dynamic method of translation. But history teaches that inconsistency in one generation becomes heterodoxy in the next. Where the dynamic method of translation is embraced, it is but one small step to the embracing of the dynamic view of inspiration as well.

It should be obvious by now that my counsel is that we should use formal equivalence translations and promote them among the people of God. While dynamic translations may have value, they should not be used as our primary study Bibles or as the standards from which we derive our personal or corporate theology and practice. It is also probably unwise to use them as pulpit Bibles or as pew Bibles, because in doing so they are invested with the aura of the approval of the church.

The NIV is not worthy of becoming the standard version of the English-speaking world. Its accuracy is suspect in too many ways. This conclusion may not be welcome in some quarters and some no doubt are convinced that they have good reasons for drawing the opposite conclusion. I can only say that I have not reached this conclusion hastily. Moreover, I have written with a clear conscience that I have been fair to the men who produced the NIV. In the final analysis, the reader must judge for himself whether the NIV deserves the place which its publishers seek for it.

In closing, I must make one final observation. We must beware of the long-term costs of supposed short-term gains. The idea in some places seems to be that more people will read their Bibles if they have one of the simpler dynamic translations, like the NIV. This may or may not be so; I do not know. I suspect that spiritually-minded folk have always read their Bibles and studied diligently those parts 'hard to be understood' (*2 Peter 3:16*). I do know, however, that sacrificing precision for simplicity is no bargain. Inaccurate and paraphrastic Bible translations cannot but contribute to the further erosion of theological precision in the decades to come.

Many new versions have come from the press in the twentieth century and undoubtedly we may expect more in the future. Each will claim to be the 'new standard in Bible translation'. We cannot afford to be swept along by the advertising or by the flurry of uncritical enthusiasm which accompanies each new Bible version. We must be cautious and conservative. We must insist that new versions earn their right to widespread use in the churches not by advertising finesse but by our careful scrutiny of their accuracy. The Bible is the touchstone of our faith and practice. We cannot afford to be careless and uninformed in these matters.

Appendix A

The Revision of the NIV

As noted above, my research was confined to the text published in *The NIV Study Bible* (1985). This was the latest edition available when my research began. I chose it because it represented the latest fruit of the labours of the Committee on Bible Translation of the International Bible Society. It would have been fundamentally unfair for me to have criticized older editions of the NIV, when revisions were already in print.

The nature and the extent of past revisions to the NIV are important, however, since they probably reflect to a significant degree the principles which will prevail in future revisions by the Committee. The International Bible Society in East Brunswick, New Jersey kindly provided me with a list of the passages where revisions have been made. According to the documents which I received from the Society, there have been three sets of revisions adopted (as of August 1987). In the summer of 1983 the Committee made approximately 930 changes which they labelled as 'limited revisions'.[1] In November 1985, sixteen additional changes were made; and in November 1986, nine more revisions were added.

The revisions are of different sorts. Some are revisions of footnotes, sectional headings, titles (in the *Psalms*), and textual superscripts. Others are matters of punctuation (e.g., from 'came about.' to 'came about:' at *Matthew 1:18*) or verse division (e.g., *Acts 8:18–19*). Still others are matters of spelling (e.g., 'Moloch' to 'Molech' at *Acts 7:43* and 'fellow man' to 'fellowman' at *Romans 13:8*) or matters of style (e.g., 'even granted' to 'granted even' at *Acts 11:18* and 'one' to 'One' at *Matthew 10:28*).

[1] Approximately 315 were in the New Testament; the rest in the Old Testament.

[71]

A large group of the revisions are the substitution of word equivalents (e.g., 'dumb' to 'mute' at *Matthew 9:33* and 'house-tops' to 'roofs' at *Luke 12:3*). At a number of places there appears to be an attempt to give a rendering closer to the original text (e.g., 'Out of my sight' to 'Get behind me' at *Mark 8:33* and 'is' to 'will be' at *Luke 15:7*); at other places, however, the revisions have produced a text further from the original (e.g., 'As I live' to 'As surely as I live' at *Romans 14:11* and 'this man's' to 'his' at *John 18:17*).

In some places the revisions restore the grammatical subordination of the original (e.g., at *Acts 19:11–12*, 'God did extraordinary miracles through Paul. Handkerchiefs and aprons that had touched him were taken to the sick' to 'God did extraordinary miracles through Paul, so that even handkerchiefs and aprons that had touched him were taken to the sick'). This kind of revision, however, was not widespread. In some places brackets were removed (e.g., '[manna]' to 'manna' at *John 6:58*); at other places brackets were added (e.g., 'It was meant' to '[It was intended]' at *John 12:7*).

All in all, the Committee's label 'limited revisions' is accurate. Although the 1983 changes were numerous, for the most part they were superficial and do not reflect a major change of translation philosophy on the part of the Committee. The same is true of the 1985 and 1986 changes. The kind of revision, of course, needed to make the NIV accurate in terms of formal equivalence would be quite extensive. Such a revision virtually would produce a new translation with only limited resemblance to the present NIV. Unless there is a fundamental change of translation philosophy, revision on that scale will not be forthcoming. While revisions will probably be made to the text of the NIV in the future, I personally expect them to follow the general pattern of past revisions.

∾ Appendix B ∾

Archaic Language and Translation Philosophy

Some writers, in the course of praising dynamic equivalence translations in contrast to the 'hard to read' formal equivalence versions, complain about the archaic language of the King James Version. We must be careful, however, not to confuse archaic language and translation philosophy. Strictly speaking, archaic language is not the product of formal equivalence principles. A dynamic equivalence translation produced in the same century would suffer from the same archaisms as the KJV. Philosophy of translation is not here the issue; therefore, when we encounter archaic language in the KJV (and to a lesser degree in the ASV), any lack of clarity to the modern reader because of these archaisms is not to be put to the account of the philosophy of formal equivalence.

We cannot, however, simply dismiss the fact that the KJV and (to a lesser degree) the ASV contain archaisms. The question is: Is the KJV so archaic as to be useless or even dangerous to this generation?[1] Some apparently think so. Kubo and Specht assert:

To the younger generation it is quite clear that the KJV, for all its literary beauty, is hopelessly out of date. It may still speak to the Bible lover of the older generation who has become familiar with its sixteenth-century English, but for the majority of English-speaking people its language has become almost a foreign tongue. There is grave danger that the continued use of this version may give modern

[1]The case against the ASV is not impressive. Although the ASV contains some archaisms (e.g., 'thee' and 'thou'), most of the archaisms of the KJV were modernized by the revisers. For the most part, the vocabulary of the ASV is still in current usage.

man the impression that the Bible belongs to another age, and that it is irrelevant to the twentieth century.[1]

This surely is an overstatement. The 'older generation' in question did not grow up speaking sixteenth-century English. As Kubo and Specht note, though it was a form of the English language different from what they used in their daily lives, the 'older generation' became familiar with it because a book which was very important to them was written in it. Moreover, just because the Bible came to them with some archaic language, they were not confused by an impression that the Bible belonged just to another age. They were twentieth-century people who knew that the Bible, even in an old translation, was very relevant to their modern world.

Now I am not proposing that we force the KJV on the present or future generations; but neither am I prepared to keep it from them. We should encourage people to use accurate versions in modern English; however, we should not insist that they avoid the KJV (or the ASV) just because some expert thinks that the style and vocabulary is beyond them. While Elizabethan English and archaic vocabulary may cause problems for children and others with very limited reading skills, the average literate adult adjusts to the Elizabethan style in a relatively brief time and can discover the meaning of the archaic words with relatively little effort (if he is willing to make the effort) from the context or from a good dictionary.

[1]Sakae Kubo and Walter Specht, *So Many Versions?* (Grand Rapids: Zondervan Publishing House, 1975), pp. 200–201.

Appendix C ❧

The Textus Receptus and the Text of the New Testament

The question of the original form of the text of the New Testament continues to be the subject of careful study by biblical scholars. The importance of such study especially can be seen when we recall that the orthodox doctrine of divine inspiration (i.e., verbal-plenary inspiration) and the doctrine of biblical inerrancy and infallibility have to do with the original manuscripts of the Bible (i.e., the actual documents which came from the pens of the biblical writers, technically known as 'autographs').

The scholarly discipline which makes the study of the original form of the biblical text its special business is known as textual criticism. Textual critics are faced with two fundamental facts. First, as far as we know, none of the autographs of the New Testament has survived to our day; and even if an autograph has survived, we have no way of distinguishing it from later copies. Second, the approximately five thousand Greek manuscripts of all or part of the New Testament contain textual differences at some places (technically known as 'variant readings' or 'variants'). On first consideration these facts may appear to cast doubt over the reliability of the Greek manuscripts from which our English translations were made; but when we understand the situation more clearly, we can appreciate Machen's observation that the study of the manuscripts is a wonderfully reassuring thing. In the interest of laying unwarranted doubts to rest, two basic observations need to be made before proceeding.

First, compared to what the manuscripts have in common, the number of variant readings having significant interpretive importance is small. The degree of total agreement between the ancient manuscripts of the New Testament is extraordinary. And at those places where the manuscripts do differ, most of the variations are matters of word order, spelling, number (singular or plural), person (first, second, or third), tense of verbs, substitution of synonyms, etc. Another significant group of variants can easily be identified as having arisen from the faulty eyesight or hearing of scribes who were making copies. Only a very few variants are of significant interpretive importance. It is critical that we recognize this. Not all instances of variation are of equal importance; and once the mass of relatively inconsequential variants is set aside, a whole new picture of the textual situation emerges, one which does not cast doubt over the reliability of the textual basis of our English translations.

Second, it is a truth often repeated, though usually not enough appreciated, that no doctrine of the faith rests upon a variant reading as its sole foundation.[1] Even if we were to eliminate the testimony of every passage where textual variation occurs, the great doctrines of the faith would remain secure.

The Bible is the sole legitimate source of the church's doctrine. Textual criticism's task is to identify, at the places in the manuscript evidence where variant readings occur, the original text of the Bible. This being so, then it follows that, far from being an enemy of truth, where its task is pursued using sound principles, textual criticism is the friend of truth and a valuable aid to the church in drawing the precise boundaries of 'biblical' faith and practice.[2]

In the opinion of some conservative Christians, the application of the principles of textual criticism to the text of the New

[1]This has been recognized by textual critics since the very infancy of the modern period of textual criticism. J. A. Bengel (1687–1752) seems to be the first forcefully to have made this point. The conclusion of Kenyon often has been echoed: 'No fundamental point of doctrine rests upon a disputed reading: and the truths of Christianity are as certainly expressed in the text of Westcott and Hort as in that of Stephanus.' Frederic G. Kenyon, *Handbook to the Textual Criticism of the New Testament* (London: Macmillan and Co., Limited, 1908), p. 317.

[2]As Clark observes, 'Textual criticism plays its part at the very center of the Church's doctrine.' Kenneth W. Clark, 'Textual Criticism and Doctrine,' in *Studia Paulina In Honorem Johannis De Swaan Septuagenarii*, ed. J. H. Sevenster and W. C. Van Unnik (Haarlem: De Erven F. Bohn N.V., 1953), p. 55.

Testament is unnecessary, since in their view the Greek text used by the translators of the King James Version (the so-called Textus Receptus, or Received Text) represents exactly the inerrant and infallible original autographs of the New Testament. The expression of this view frequently is accompanied with the charge that emendation of the Received Text, by the substitution of variant readings from other manuscripts of the New Testament, is nothing less than tampering with the Word of God which our Lord providentially has preserved throughout all the centuries since the inspired documents were written. Furthermore, any translation based on a text at variance from the Received Text automatically is condemned because of its supposedly corrupt foundation. Appeal is often made to Psalm 12:6–7 and Matthew 5:18, with the assertion being made that these promises are fulfilled in the Textus Receptus.

Many other conservative Christians, however, who also believe in verbal-plenary inspiration and biblical inerrancy and infallibility, dissent from the opinion that God's promise to preserve His Word has been fulfilled exclusively in the Textus Receptus. Where there are variant readings in the extant manuscripts of the Scriptures, these Christians seek to determine, through the application of sound principles of textual criticism, which readings were penned by the biblical writers and which readings came into existence through other means.

Sadly, some are not content to debate in the arena of biblical science, but resort to arguing *ad hominem*. It is all too common to find men resorting to innuendo and even to vilification in an attempt to subdue their scholarly opponents. On the one hand, it is common for those who disagree with the 'Textus Receptus only' folk to be vilified as heretics. On the other hand, it is a matter of course in many academic circles to lampoon defenders of the Textus Receptus (or their near relatives, the advocates of the Majority Text) as unscholarly obscurantists bent on defending a lost cause, and to caricature them as having a mentality compatible with membership in the Flat Earth Society. Such blanket categorizing is both unwarranted and unkind. It is true that some of the advocates of the Textus Receptus are uncritical in their thinking and make extreme claims in their zeal to overturn opposing views; but the same also can be said of some who advocate an eclectic text. One would hope that the principle would be too axiomatic to require stating, but apparently such is not the case: personal attack upon the character of one's scholarly opponent is the last defence of a man devoid of sound arguments.

Actually, in the field of New Testament textual criticism, there are four competing schools of thought: (1) the Textus Receptus only folk; (2) the advocates of the Majority Text[1]; (3) the heirs of Westcott–Hort, who seek to evaluate external evidence[2] as well as internal evidence[3] in selecting among variant readings; (4) the so-called Radical Eclectics, who depend almost exclusively on internal evidence when making textual judgments. Each of these camps operates on the basis of numerous assumptions which are open to debate. Each is guilty of a certain amount of bias and subjectivity, as well as a great deal of over-simplification of the textual issue, all their protests to the contrary notwithstanding. Each would profit from more open-mindedness and less dogmatism. All would profit from noting the observation of A. E. Housman:

Textual criticism is not a branch of mathematics, nor indeed an exact science at all. . . . A textual critic engaged upon his business is not at all like Newton investigating the motions of the planets: he is much more like a dog hunting for fleas. If a dog hunted for fleas on mathematical principles, basing his researches on statistics of area and population, he would never catch a flea except by accident. They require to be treated as individuals; and every problem which presents itself to the textual critic must be regarded as possibly unique.[4]

It is not this writer's purpose to enter into a detailed description of the various tenets of the competing text critical schools. My

[1]The advocates of the Majority Text position recently have published an edition of the Greek New Testament which reflects the fruit of their text-critical labours. See Zane Hodges and Arthur Farstad, eds., *The Greek New Testament According to the Majority Text* (Nashville: Thomas Nelson, 1982).

[2]Such things as age, geographical distribution, and genealogical or family relationships of manuscripts.

[3]Internal evidence is basically of two sorts: (1) transcriptional probabilities, having to do with paleographical matters and the habits of the scribes who copied the documents of the New Testament; and (2) intrinsic probabilities, having to do with what the original author was more likely to have written.

[4]Quoted by Bruce M. Metzger, *The Text of the New Testament* (New York: Oxford University Press, 1968), p. 219.

purpose solely is to challenge the opinion that the Textus Receptus represents at every point the original documents of the New Testament and, therefore, that it is tampering with the Word of God ever to give preference to variant readings from other manuscript evidence for the text of the New Testament.

The Textus Receptus, of course, is not a single ancient handwritten manuscript of the Greek New Testament (like Codex Sinaiticus or Codex Alexandrinus), but a printed edition which itself underwent revision both before and after the label 'Received Text' was attached to it. This fact alone casts doubt over the assertion that the Textus Receptus should never be emended or any of its readings challenged. Perhaps a brief history will help to put the Textus Receptus in proper perspective.

The first printed edition of the Greek New Testament was part of a work known as the Complutensian Polyglot, produced in 1514 under the sponsorship of Cardinal Ximenes of Spain (although it was not offered to the public until 1522). It has never been satisfactorily determined which Greek manuscripts of the New Testament formed the basis of this edition. Ximenes, however, in his dedication to Pope Leo X, said: 'For Greek copies indeed we are indebted to your Holiness, who sent us most kindly from the apostolic library very ancient codices, both of the Old and the New Testament; which have aided us very much in this undertaking.' Ximenes' reference probably was to manuscripts from the Vatican library.

The first printed Greek testament actually placed on the market was prepared by Desiderius Erasmus of Rotterdam and published in 1516. Apparently eager to be the first to offer to the public a printed edition of the Greek New Testament, the German publisher Johann Froben prevailed on Erasmus to prepare an edition suitable for publication. Erasmus travelled to Basle and, using only the manuscripts available to him in that city, produced the edition requested. Printing began three months after Erasmus' arrival in Basle and within the year the project was complete. Later Erasmus would reflect on the haste with which this edition was produced and comment that it was 'precipitated rather than edited'.

Since Erasmus had no manuscript which contained the entire New Testament, he edited several together into an eclectic text. None of the manuscripts that he used dated before the twelfth century. At several places in the text of Revelation, where verses were either missing from the manuscript from which he was working or where the text was uncertain, Erasmus translated the Latin Vulgate into Greek. The result of Erasmus' self-made Greek text at these places was that he produced a number of readings that have never been found in any known Greek manuscript, but which are still found in editions of the Textus Receptus today.[1]

Erasmus issued five editions of his Greek testament. The second edition was the basis of Luther's German translation. The third edition was the first in which he included the so-called *Comma Johanneum* at 1 John 5:7–8. The fourth and fifth editions reflect a major revision in which Erasmus emended his text to conform at many places to the Complutensian Polyglot.[2]

Before leaving the work of Erasmus, a brief word concerning the *Comma Johanneum* at 1 John 5:7–8 seems in order. When his first edition appeared, Erasmus was criticized by some because the text did not include the words: 'the Father, the Word, and the Holy Ghost: and these three are one. And there are three that bear witness in earth' (KJV translation). These words were found in many of the editions of the Latin Vulgate current in Erasmus' day. Erasmus promised that he would include the disputed words in future editions if a single Greek manuscript could be found which contained them. At length such a manuscript was presented to him. Erasmus kept his promise and placed the words in his third edition, although in a lengthy footnote he expressed his suspicion that the manuscript had been fabricated deliberately for the occasion. He omitted the words from his subsequent editions. The manuscript in question (now designated as Greg. 61 and as Codex Montfortianus) now resides at Trinity College, Dublin; and, as Metzger notes, it 'opens almost of its own accord at 1 John v – so often has it been consulted at this passage!'[3]

The French publisher Robert Estienne (also known as Stephanus or Stephens) published four editions of the Greek New Testament between 1546 and 1551. His first two editions were drawn from the Complutensian Polyglot and from the Erasmian editions. His third edition (1550) was the first Greek New Testament to include variant readings from other manuscripts in a

---

[1]For examples, see Metzger, p. 100.
[2]For example, in Revelation about ninety passages were emended.
[3]Metzger, p. 101.

critical apparatus. This edition became the received text of many, especially in England. The 1550 edition still is printed by some as the 'Textus Receptus',[1] although the title itself actually was used first with reference to a modified form of the Stephanus text published by the Elzevir brothers in 1633. Stephanus' fourth edition was the first to appear with verse divisions.

Theodore Beza, perhaps best remembered as the associate of John Calvin, published nine editions of the Greek New Testament between 1565 and 1604. Although Beza included readings from Codex Bezae, from Codex Claromontanus, and from other Greek manuscript sources, generally he followed the Stephanus text and helped to popularize it. Beza's edition of 1598 is the 'primary authority' cited as the basis for the Trinitarian Bible Society's current printing of the 'Textus Receptus'.[2]

The King James translators used as their chief sources the 1550 and 1551 editions of Stephanus and Beza's editions of 1589 and 1598. They did not, however, as is generally believed, work from a single homogeneous text known as the 'Textus Receptus'.

In 1624 the Elzevir brothers of Leiden published a small pocket edition taken mainly from Beza's 1565 edition. The preface to their second edition (1633) claims that it contains 'the text which is now received by all'.[3] From this advertising 'blurb' (as Metzger calls it) arose the designation 'Textus Receptus'. As the Stephanus edition (1550) had become the received text of Great Britain, so the Elzevir text (1633) became the received text of the Continent.

As seems clear from the history of the Textus Receptus, the title does not designate a single edition of the Greek New Testament but a family of editions which differ from one another at certain points.[4] This being so, to this writer it seems indefensible to assert that the Textus Receptus alone preserves the pure Word of God and, therefore, is not to be emended by the substitution of variant readings from other, more ancient texts. For which 'Textus Receptus' is this claim made? For Erasmus' third edition (1522)?

[1] See George Ricker Berry, *The Interlinear Literal Translation of the Greek New Testament* (Grand Rapids: Zondervan Publishing House, 1958), p. ii.

[2] See the *Preface* of *The New Testament: The Greek Text Underlying the English Authorised Version of 1611* (London: The Trinitarian Bible Society, n.d.).

[3] *Textum ergo habes, nunc ab omnibus receptum.*

[4] For example, the Stephanus edition of 1550 and the Elzevir edition of 1633 differ from one another in 287 places.

For Stephanus' third edition (1550)? For Beza's eighth edition (1598)? Or for the Elzevirs' second edition (1633)? Which 'Textus Receptus' is to be guarded against the so-called attacks of textual critics? If the history of the Textus Receptus itself is a history of revision, why is it beyond revision today? At what point in history did it become immune to the process which characterized its production? If it was open to revision and correction when the body of textual evidence was relatively small, why is it now closed to that process when the textual evidence is far more extensive?

Some may be disturbed by my remarks. But are we not under obligation before God to acknowledge what is patently true? God has preserved every word of the inspired Scriptures – we defend that principle as vigorously as the advocates of the Textus Receptus; however, He has not done so solely in the Textus Receptus. While it is true that for the most part (indeed, in overwhelming proportions) the text of the New Testament is free from variations, there yet remain those places where the manuscripts differ. This reality means that at those places, we must earnestly pray and study to know which words among the variations came from God by inspiration. At such times especially, humble men know their own inadequacy and cast themselves on the kindness of God, seeking His guidance.

Having read the preceding remarks, the reader may be tempted to conclude that I am arguing that the Textus Receptus is in some way dangerous. This is not the case. Although there are differences from what some might regard as a purer text, these differences should not be blown out of proportion. The Textus Receptus is a dependable guide for the people of God and has shed blessed light on the path of many pilgrims on their way to the celestial city. And the same can be said for the King James Version, which is still one of the finest translations of the Scriptures ever produced in any language. My purpose merely is to ask that no unique or exclusive place be given to the Textus Receptus or to the King James Version, to the exclusion of other safe guides in the Scriptures.

Index of Authors

Index of Scripture References